A SHORT HISTORY OF THE ROYAL MARINES

1664 - 2019

EDITED BY
COLONEL B L CARTER OBE
(HON EDITOR RMHS)

ROYAL MARINES HISTORICAL SOCIETY SPECIAL PUBLICATION NO 48

First Edition 2002 (reprinted 2003)
Second Revised Edition 2004
Third Revised Edition 2008
Fourth Revised Edition 2013
Fifth Revised Edition 2019

Printed by Holbrooks Printers, Norway road, Portsmouth, Hants. PO3 5HX
© RMHS 2019

ISBN 978 1 908123 18 3

RM Historical Society, NMRN, HM Naval Base, Portsmouth P01 3NH
www.nmrn.org.uk

Introduction

This fifth, updated edition has been produced by the Royal Marines Historical Society as a compact historical guide to the Royal Marines for easy reference. It includes extensive appendices covering many aspects of Corps history. The RMHS is most grateful to the RMA-The Royal Marines Charity for its most generous donation towards the costs of the production of this Short History.

All photographs are Crown copyright or the copyright of the National Museum of the Royal Navy and permission to use any of them must be obtained through the Museum. Our thanks to the late Charles Stadden, a member of the Society, for his approval to use paintings which were originally commissioned by the Royal Marines Museum. Thanks again go to Captain Derek Oakley MBE, Major Alastair Donald, Major Mark Bentinck and, particularly for this edition, the current Corps Historian, Lieutenant Colonel George Gelder, who did most of the updating of the text and the pictures; also to the Corps Secretary, Lieutenant Colonel Ed Musto for ensuring that the appendices were up to date and finally to Tim Mitchell for his excellent design work and professional advice; and to members of the serving Corps for help with more recent history up to and including the campaigns in Iraq and Afghanistan.

There are large numbers of published books relating to the history of the Royal Marines since 1664, most of which are available for deeper research in the Corps archives at the National Museum of the Royal Navy, Portsmouth. A selected bibliography is at Appendix U.

The Royal Marines Historical Society would like to acknowledge the following authors whose works were used extensively in this booklet: General Sir H E Blumberg, Colonel C Field, Colonel G Grover, A Cecil Hampshire, James D Ladd, Major General J M Moulton, Capt D A Oakley, Colonel Markham Rose, Peter C Smith and Major General J H A Thompson.

The Royal Marines Historical Society was formed in 1964 and carries out research into all aspects of Corps history, working closely with the RM Museum. It publishes newsletters, journals and books (Special Publications).

Meticulous readers will find some inconsistencies in the abbreviations of ranks and the words 'Marines' and 'marines', but continuous use of 'Royal Marines' is too cumbersome. The authors have taken liberties as they deemed appropriate.

Contents

Genealogical Tree of The Royal Marines

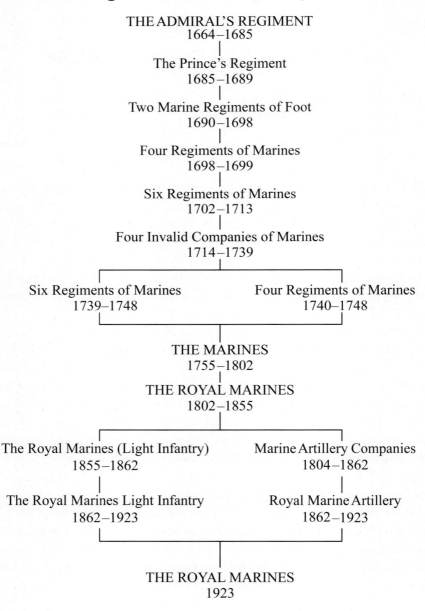

THE ADMIRAL'S REGIMENT
1664–1685

The Prince's Regiment
1685–1689

Two Marine Regiments of Foot
1690–1698

Four Regiments of Marines
1698–1699

Six Regiments of Marines
1702–1713

Four Invalid Companies of Marines
1714–1739

| Six Regiments of Marines 1739–1748 | Four Regiments of Marines 1740–1748 |

THE MARINES
1755–1802

THE ROYAL MARINES
1802–1855

| The Royal Marines (Light Infantry) 1855–1862 | Marine Artillery Companies 1804–1862 |
| The Royal Marines Light Infantry 1862–1923 | Royal Marine Artillery 1862–1923 |

THE ROYAL MARINES
1923

Foreword to the Fifth
Revised Edition
By Major General Julian Thompson CB OBE

We have compelled every land and every sea to open up a path for our valour, and have everywhere planted eternal memorials of our friendship and our enmity.

Pericles

The Author of a history of the Royal Marines compared us with the French Foreign Legion, remarking that both gained their reputations after years of gruelling service in far corners of the world, often unheard, unseen, and too frequently unappreciated. The Royal Marines and the Foreign Legion are famous for their ability to turn their hands to anything. The unofficial motto of the Legion, which might be translated; 'get yourself out of the mess because no else is going to', could equally have applied to the Royal Marines many times in what Winston Churchill called 'their long, rough, glorious history'.

The first edition of the Short History of the Royal Marines was published in 2002. The Corps has been so busy over the subsequent seventeen years that four more editions have been required to keep pace with events, hence this one, the Fifth. To have fitted 355 busy years of Royal Marines operations and activity into 200 pages is no mean feat on the part of Brian Carter. As well as bringing the story up to the year 2019, this edition, like its predecessors, contains a wealth of information on the traditions and many other aspects of Corps life that will continue to provide answers to the most searching questions, not only those aimed by instructors at recruits under training, but also to enlighten the general public and provide a handy reminder for any serving or retired Royal Marines, however senior.

We live in an age in which many, especially in the media and other opinion-forming bodies, denigrate the past as mere sentiment at best and an unwelcome bar to progress at worst. While it is true that past performance is no guarantee of future execution, and mere imitation of one's predecessor's actions and methods may be unproductive, standards and ethos can be a guide when in danger or in doubt. Generations of our predecessors have 'been there' before; whether on the bullet-swept decks of ships under sail, in the turrets and transmitting stations of warships in both World Wars, wading ashore in numerous landings with the cold sea behind and potential disaster staring them in the face, in helicopters, landing craft and amphibians of many kinds, and in the end so often in what a United States Marine called 'LPCs' or 'leather personnel carriers', boots, 'yomping' to close with the enemy in every kind of terrain imaginable from the beaches of Normandy to the landing zones of the El Faw Peninsula, and the demanding and often lethal terrain of Afghanistan.

The final chapter of this new edition provides an excellent summary of the Corp's contribution to the Afghanistan campaign, and the diversity of the skills that the Royal Marines brought to it. In doing so it covers an aspect that is little-known, especially by the public, the gallantry and professionalism of Royal Marines aviators; in both Harriers and helicopters. This chapter also gives the reader a concise account of the many other operations carried out since 2013 (the date of the previous edition), with a glimpse of the Corps's future roles and challenges.

The RM Memorial in the Mall, London, which was rededicated in 2000 as the RM National memorial to commemorate also over two hundred Royal Marines killed on active service all around the globe since The Second World War

'Meet', said Winston Churchill, introducing one of his Royal Marine bodyguards to the US President Roosevelt, 'a member of the greatest Corps in the World'. The outstanding young people joining the Corps today are but the most recent inheritors of a tradition in which to give one's all to achieve the objective is ingrained and to whom failure is not an option. On occasions, disaster, chaos, yes; our past does not lack examples of these, but stories of how Royal Marines have risen above these abound, and many are covered in this book. I commend it to all serving and ex-Royal Marines as well as to the general public who may find the story of the greatest Corps in the World of interest.

Chapter 1

The Early Marine Regiments
1664 – 1755

The Royal Marines are the soldiers of the Royal Navy and can trace their descent from a regiment specially raised and trained for service with the Navy and paid by the Admiralty.

It was at the outbreak of the Second Dutch War in 1664 that a regiment of 1,200 men, commanded by Colonel Sir William Killigrew, was ordered to be formed in the City of London. The men were recruited for service to the 'Navy Royall and Admiralty' and the regiment was named after the Lord High Admiral himself, Charles II's brother, James, who was fitting out a fleet to face the Dutch in Home waters. Defined as 'Land Souldjers' the regiment was known as the Duke of York and Albany's Maritime Regiment of Foot and the Order in Council was dated 28 October 1664.

James was a strict disciplinarian and welcomed a regiment that would help with his manning problem and bring personal loyalty to the fleet. It had been the practice for two hundred years for ships of the Royal Navy to be paid off in peace and crews impressed from the seafaring population in times of emergency. When war was declared in February 1665, the English Fleet sailed under James and met the Dutch off Lowestoft in a fierce battle that left both fleets incapable of further action. This was the first action by the new regiment who were strikingly arrayed in uniforms of yellow coats with red facings, sashes and stockings and were all armed with flintlock muskets, instead of some with pikes as in other regiments. Yellow was the favourite colour of the Duke.

It was often known as The Admiral's Regiment, until James was forced to resign as Lord High Admiral in 1673, when his Regiment became referred to as The Duke's Regiment. The Colonel was licensed by the Lord Mayor of London to recruit from within the City and many were from the Trained Bands, the City's own volunteer militia. It is from this origin that the Royal Marines today derive the privilege, enjoyed by very few regiments, of marching through the City with Colours flying, drums beating and bayonets fixed. The first use of the

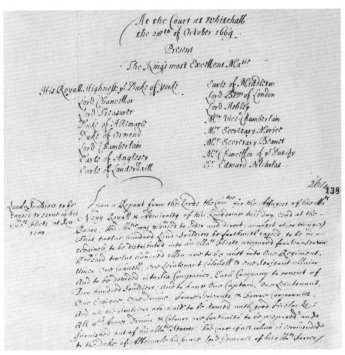

Privy Council Proceedings authorising 1,200 soldiers to be raised
for sea service.

term 'Marines' that has been traced is in a letter written by Captain Sylas Taylor of the regiment in 1672 after the Battle of Solebay.

When Charles II died in 1685, his brother came to the throne as James II and the Regiment passed to Prince George, James's son-in-law and the husband of his second daughter, Anne. The Regiment was titled Prince George of Denmark's Maritime Regiment, but better known as The Prince's Regiment. However James's reign as a Catholic king was short lived and William of Orange was invited to England in the Protestant cause. Many Army regiments went over to William, but the Prince's Regiment, commanded by an ardent royalist for over twenty years, remained loyal to James. After he fled to France in 1689, William with his wife Mary, James's eldest daughter, were declared joint sovereigns. The Regiment was considered to be too favourable to the previous regime and consequently disbanded, its men being incorporated into the Coldstream Guards.

Almost immediately Britain was again at war with France, and the following year two Marine Regiments were raised by the Earls of Torrington and Pembroke as the 1st and 2nd Regiments of Marines. Although the men of these Regiments served in the Fleet in all the sea battles of the war, ashore in Jamaica, at the siege of Cork in Ireland and in France, after the Peace of Ryswick, both regiments were disbanded in 1699.

The War of the Spanish Succession broke out in 1702 and a number of regiments were raised, six of them as Marines and each known by the name of their Colonel, Saunderson's, Villiers's, Fox's, Mordaunt's, Holt's and Shannon's. These regiments fought in Spain, France and North America and most of them were involved, with 400 Dutch Marines, in the Capture and Defence of Gibraltar in 1704, of which a contemporary author wrote "The garrison did more than could be humanly expected and the British Marines gained immortal honour". At the Treaty of Utrecht in 1713, the last three regiments were disbanded, while the first three were reformed as line infantry, later becoming the East Lancashire Regiment, the East Surrey Regiment and the Duke of Cornwall's Light Infantry, and all of which are justly proud of their origins as Marines.

Once again there were no Regiments of Marines. From the time of the accession of George I in 1714, it was only four companies of Marine invalids which kept the name alive. Formed for garrison duties, the companies were found from men of the former Marine Regiments, who were no longer fit for active service.

It was not until 1739, when war with Spain broke out again (known as the War of Jenkin's Ear), that Marines properly reappeared on the scene. When George II addressed Parliament and announced that "*In the prosecution of this war a number of soldiers to serve on board the fleet may be requisite, and I have judged it proper that a body of Marines should be raised*", it was greeted with loud applause. Six Regiments of Marines were formed in 1739 and were joined by another four Regiments in 1740. During almost the whole of the next decade Marines experienced highs and lows, fighting in the Caribbean, including the disastrous attack on Cartagena, they sailed round the world with Anson, during the 1745 Rebellion they were at Culloden, and in India they took part in the Siege of Pondicherry, where the well-documented female Marine, Hannah Snell, was severely wounded (*see her memoirs on page 11*).

The capture of Gibraltar by British and Dutch Marines in 1704.

Service in the Marines had become unpopular; by 1745 when a first commission cost only £250–£280 compared to the £500 for Officers of the Line. The Admiralty budget for 1747–48 provided for 40,000 seamen and 11,550 Marines. Although the Peace of Aix-la-Chapelle, signed in 1748, was merely a temporary truce in the long conflict with France, the Marine Regiments were nevertheless again disbanded.

This was the last time they were disbanded, for what had become known as the War of the Austrian Succession had finally emphasised a requirement that had built up over the eighty or so years during most of which Marines had existed. It had shown the necessity for a permanent body of troops specially raised and equipped for sea service. This force was required in order to provide landing parties from ships to destroy enemy fleets inshore, to engage in combined operations and to provide protection ashore whenever the fleet needed to take on provisions or water in unfriendly territory. It was also realised that there was an administrative factor to be addressed. At this time sailors were not usually paid until the end of the commission whereas soldiers were normally clothed and regularly paid by the Colonel of the Regiment. However when an Army regiment

Hannah Snell published her memoirs of service.

was split up among ships of the Fleet, this was seldom possible. Consequently it was necessary to have a force organised with sufficiently elastic administration to compete with these requirements. Admiral Lord Anson pressed for the formation of a permanent body of Marines under Admiralty control and organised on a company basis.

The historian G M Trevelyan wrote:

> 'It is remarkable how soon they (the Marines) acquired two reputations that clung to them for many generations – a reputation for good, honest service and character, and a reputation among snobs of being socially less smart than the Army.'

Chapter 2

Three Grand Divisions
1755 – 1827

In 1755, as war clouds again began to threaten, Parliament voted an establishment of five thousand Marines and with Lord Anson as First Lord of the Admiralty, an Order-in-Council provided for fifty independent companies organised into three Divisions at the naval ports of Chatham, Portsmouth and Plymouth. This new organisation set the pattern for the future of the Corps and lasted up until after the Second World War. Many of the experienced Officers and some of the NCOs for the first of these companies had served in the regiments disbanded in 1748. Officers were now commissioned into a definite company, recruiting parties were sent out from the Divisions and in due course detachments were sent off to sea with, it must be said, very little training at that time. These detachments varied in size from a hundred in a first-rate ship of the line, down to twenty in a small frigate.

The Seven Years War with France broke out the following year, but when Byng was sent with a Fleet to relieve Minorca and for the raids that were being made on the French coast, there were not enough Marines to go round and Army regiments had to be embarked. However, by 1758 the strength of the Marines had been increased to 14,845 in one hundred companies and Marines then served in Boscawen's fleet off Lagos, with Hawke at Quiberon Bay and in an amphibious operation they captured Senegal. Later that year, led by James Wolfe, who had been first commissioned in one of the previous Marine Regiments in 1741, they fought at Cape Breton and St John's, thus giving the French good reason to doubt their own future in Canada. Eventually at Quebec a battalion of Marines, which included Robert Ross, who was later to play a leading role in Australia, created a diversion and allowed Wolfe's force to scale the Heights of Abraham and capture the city, thereby securing Canada for Britain.

The increased strength of the Marines allowed two battalions of Marines, one from barracks and one from the Fleet to be formed during Keppel's expedition to Belleisle in 1761. They played a decisive part in the capture of this island off the coast of France on 7 June. On 22 April, after an earlier landing had failed, Grenadiers of the 19th Regiment and a company of Marines scaled the cliffs at La Maria in a diversionary attack. Although fiercely attacked by the French, they held their positions until relieved by the remainder of the battalion. This then became the main landing and the French defences were overrun. Asked afterwards what troops have been most effective against them the French replied 'les petits grenadiers', meaning the Marines who wore grenadier caps but who were not as tall as the men in Army grenadier companies. It was subsequently written *"The Marines gained immortal glory..."* and it is believed that the laurel wreath, which forms part of the insignia of the Corps, was awarded to honour the part played by the Marines in the capture of Belleisle, and which today is one of the memorable dates celebrated by the Corps (*see Appendix B*).

By the time Spain entered the war in 1762, the voted strength had gradually risen to over 19,000, and it was the new and far more flexible organisation that enabled the Admiralty to manage the administration of this expansion by gradually increasing the number of companies at each of the three Divisions, and which by then had reached an overall total of 135. This ultimately must have provided sufficient detachments at sea, because it was possible to form two further battalions which were engaged in the capture of Havana.

Around the Globe with Napoleon: 1770–1815

The Seven Years War had left France waiting to avenge her defeat and the American colonists, relieved of the French threat from Canada, were able to express their resentment of home authority by resorting to violence. In 1773 the famous Boston Tea Party was the climax of the American colonists' resistance to British taxation and led them to sever the ties with the mother country two years later with the American Revolution.

A Marine battalion under Major Pitcairn was sent to Boston and on 19 April 1775 the opening shots of the American War of Independence were fired by a detachment of his Marines at Lexington. Further Marines arrived in May and were formed into another battalion. After seeing action at Lexington and Concord, some 750 Marines reached Boston on 20 May. Here they were formed into two battalions, the 1st Marines under Major Short and the 2nd Marines commanded by Major Tupper, with Major John Pitcairn in overall command.

Bunker Hill, taken by the Marines and the 47th Regiment in 1775.

On 17 June they were engaged in driving the rebels from their positions on the top of Bunker Hill at the point of the bayonet. In the closing stages of the battle, in the face of a deadly volley their commander was mortally wounded. It is said that imitation is the sincerest form of flattery and therefore it must be recorded that on 10 November 1775 the Continental Congress formed a Marine Corps, a force with which today the Corps has a strong affiliation (*see Appendix K*).

On the other side of the world, a small Marine detachment was with Captain Cook when he landed at Botany Bay in 1770, but it was in 1788 that Marines started to play a major part in the founding of Australia. A large contingent of twenty-one Officers and 192 men commanded by Major Robert Ross, along with forty-five wives and children accompanied the first convicts and were present when the Union flag was raised with due ceremony at Sydney Cove. Ross became the first Lieutenant Governor of New South Wales and then of Norfolk Island. After disagreement with Governor Arthur Phillip about the poor pay and conditions of Marines he returned to England in 1791. Captain David Collins, another veteran of Bunker Hill, was appointed the Judge Advocate subsequently becoming Lieutenant Governor in Tasmania in 1803.

Marines were with Captain Cook when he claimed a British Possession at Botany Bay in 1770.

As colonisation of Australia continued, many Marines took their discharge and formed the nucleus of the first settlers.

When France declared war on Britain in 1793 following the Revolution, the Navy found itself extremely short not only of seamen, but also of Marines. In consequence a number of infantry regiments again served at sea in ships of the line, whilst Marines were mainly sent to frigates and sloops. These are the Army regiments, which today are proud of the honours and traditions they observe in their historic dates, badges, and in some cases even music, and which are derived from the time they spent at sea. Detachments of these regiments, together with those of the Marines, fought in the Battles of the Glorious First of June, Cape St Vincent and Camperdown, and shared in Nelson's victories at the Nile and Copenhagen. Indeed on 1 June 1794 when Lord Howe met and decisively defeated a similar sized French fleet, thirteen of his ships carried Marine detachments. By 1801, out of a Navy Vote of 135,000 men, nearly 23,000 were Marines, later to be increased to over 30,000. When the war was over in 1802 the Corps was reduced to 12,119.

That year was a memorable one as it was probably not only the meritorious service of the Marines that resulted in the Corps being granted the title 'Royal', but also their loyalty at the time of the great naval mutinies of Spithead and the Nore in 1797. On 29 April Lord St Vincent, First Lord of the Admiralty, announced that His Majesty King George III had been pleased to direct that in future the Corps should now be styled the 'Royal Marines'. Orders were given that their new uniforms, scarlet with blue facings, were to be delivered in time for the anniversary of the King's Birthday on 4 June. At Plymouth, when they assumed these new uniforms, a large crowd cheered when they saw them parade, the barracks were illuminated and a grand ball held in their honour. Later Lord St Vincent said:

> In obtaining for them the distinction of 'Royal' I but inefficiently did my duty. I never knew an appeal made to them for honour, courage or loyalty, that they did not more than realize my highest expectations. If ever the hour of real danger should come to England, they will be found the country's sheet anchor.

From the middle of the eighteenth century Royal Artillery detachments had been embarked to man the large mortars in bomb vessels. However, because they did not consider themselves subject to the Naval Discipline Act and would not undertake ship's duties, there was friction between them and the Naval Officers on board. By 1804 the crisis had come to a head and, largely at the instigation of Lord Nelson, an artillery company was formed at each of the Royal Marine Divisions on 18 August. When a fourth Division was established at Woolwich the following year, an artillery company was formed there also. It was not until 1862 that the Royal Marine Artillery was formed into a separate Division, and work was started on a purpose-built barracks for it at Eastney in Southsea, Hampshire and its Officers were separately listed.

Trafalgar and War with America

War had broken out again with France in May 1803 and Napoleon began to amass the Grande Armee. Once again the Navy Vote rose to 38,000 seamen and 12,000 Marines and this had trebled by 1812.

On 21 October 1805 Nelson defeated the combined French and Spanish fleets off Cape Trafalgar. Over one tenth of the Corps were serving in Nelson's fleet – eighty-four Officers and 2,783 men. Captain Adair aboard HMS Victory was shot whilst repelling boarders. Another Officer, Second Lieutenant Roteley, described the scene as being "like a hailstorm of bullets passing over our heads on the poop, where we had forty Marines with small arms." Marines fought in the rigging and on the guns. In the action three Officers and 109 men were killed with sixteen Officers and 256 men wounded. After Nelson was hit, Sergeant Secker and other Marines carried him below. When the French Admiral Villeneuve wished to surrender aboard the Bucentaure it was to an Officer of the Royal Marines, Captain James Atcherley, that he first offered his sword. Thinking this was improper Atcherley declined in favour of his Captain.

Thus Napoleon's dream of invasion had ended. But it was ten long years before peace was restored following Wellington's victory at Waterloo. Before then Marines had been involved in a large number of smaller actions both ashore and afloat. British expeditions occupied Sicily and attacked distant French, Spanish and Dutch colonies, from Cape Town to Copenhagen, from Barcelona to the Dardanelles. A Marine battalion landed on the island of Walcheren, another took Anholt in the Baltic and held it, Captain 'Fighting' Nicholls becoming the Governor. There were numerous landings, often up steep cliffs against highly motivated defenders, while acting as a covering force for the Army as at Corunna and Mondego.

When Nelson was killed at Trafalgar he was carried below by Sergeant Secker.

Finally it was when Napoleon, on boarding *Bellerophon* to be transported to the island of St Helena, inspected the RM guard that he remarked *"One might do much with 100,000 soldiers such as these"*.

Three RM battalions, each with an RMA company, were engaged in the War of 1812 with the United States of America. This war opened with a series of bloody frigate actions in which the British, having neglected gunnery since Trafalgar, were soundly beaten by the larger American frigates. It was in the first of these that a British Marine shot and killed Lieutenant Bush of the United States Marine Corps and later, when the HMS *Shannon* captured the USS *Chesapeake* off Boston *"Marine fought Marine on the decks of the Chesapeake"*. In June 1813 the 1st and 2nd Battalions, each with an artillery company, arrived from Spain. After the attack on Hampton they served in Canada where the Americans were threatening Montreal. They then saw action on Lakes Champlain and Ontario where they manned some of the gunboats. They also raided the shores of Chesapeake Bay and were with the force that defeated the Americans at Bladensburg. The Brigade Commander at Hampton, Lieutenant Colonel Charles Napier (later General Sir Charles Napier in India), recorded:

> *Never in my life have I seen soldiers like the Marine Artillery. We suffered much fatigue and hardship, but never was seen anything not admirable in these glorious soldiers. Should my life extend to antediluvian years their conduct at Little Hampton will not be forgotten by me. All honour to the memory of these brave men.*

They were present when Washington was burnt in reprisal for the American sacking of Toronto. Baltimore was then besieged and from their base on Cumberland Island they carried out raids to divert the American troops from the defence of Orleans. Meanwhile Major 'Fighting' Nicholls had landed in eastern Louisiana and raised Creek and Choctaw Indians against the Americans.

Shortly afterwards, peace was proclaimed and the Marines returned to England, arriving a few weeks after Waterloo. It had been a long and varied campaign against the Americans in which Marines had been deployed in both land and sea actions.

In 1827, when the Duke of Clarence (later King William IV), presented

Colours to each of the four Divisions their new design was similar to those of the Colours carried today and much of the insignia borne was granted by King George IV at this time (*see Appendix Y*).

HRH The Duke of Clarence.
From a painting by Sir Thomas Lawrence and A Morton.

Chapter 3

The Crimea, Boers & Boxers
1827–1902

In other minor wars that followed detachments from the Mediterranean Fleet saw action when Algiers was bombarded and burnt down in the war against piracy in 1816 and also when Marines were landed from the fleet in the battle of Navarino Bay in 1827. When Queen Victoria came to the throne a Royal Marine battalion and an artillery company were in action in Spain during the Carlist War. Soon afterwards Marines from the fleet were again landed and, reinforced from Britain to make two battalions, they fought alongside the Turks during the Turko-Egyptian War, 1839–41, to recapture Syria.

A battalion from the fleet served in the First China War in the 1840s when British shipping was threatened by fleets of Chinese war junks. The Imperial Government in Peking had banned the East India Company's opium trade and other British traders came under threat. Smuggling was tolerated on both sides, but erupted with expulsions and attacks on shipping in the Pearl River. On 23 May 1841 Captain Ellis led 380 Marines in the capture of the Bogue Forts guarding the approach to Canton and occupied Hong Kong, after which a truce was declared, an indemnity paid and the Marines re-embarked. In all about seven hundred Marines fought in the war with minor actions at Chusan, Amoy and Shanghai. The final engagement of the war involved some two hundred Marines in a blistering attack on the walled city of Chinkiang Foo.

RM detachments fought ashore in the Maori Wars in New Zealand in 1845 and smaller numbers also found themselves in operations in South America, Ireland and Burma.

Carnage in the Crimea: 1847–1855
In 1847 Parliament ended life enlistment, limiting service in the Army and Marines to twelve years with re-engagement for another twelve, later reduced to nine, to qualify for pension. The Navy also introduced continuous service by an Order in Council of 1853. In 1848 Portsmouth Division moved into Forton

Barracks at Gosport, and Woolwich Division into new barracks which had been built for them facing the Common.

In March 1854 Britain and France, coming to the rescue of the dying Turkish Empire, declared war on Russia. The fleet bombarded Odessa and in September laid siege to Sevastopol. Some four hundred Marines from the fleet occupied Eupatoria and covered the flanks of the initial landing and after the armies had marched on the city a further 2,000 Marines, and 2,400 seamen landed with 140 guns. The following month the Russians tried to cut off the Army from the main British supply port of Balaclava. Taking up their siege positions, known as Marine Heights, twenty-six guns of the RM Artillery covered the charges of both the Heavy and the Light Brigades. In early November three hundred Marines under Captain Hopkins took part in the Battle of Inkerman. During this action a party of Marines, which was clearing some caves under Sergeant Richards and Corporal Prettyjohns, was attacked. Prettyjohns seized the leading Russian and threw him back, whilst his men hurled heavy stones at the remainder and became involved in close hand-to-hand fighting. It was at this time that the Victoria Cross was instituted and Corporal Prettyjohns became the

Lieutenant Dowell and Bombadier Wilkinson about to receive their VCs from Queen Victoria.

21

first of three Royal Marines to be decorated with this coveted award during the Crimean War.

At the same time, on the northern flank of Russia, another British fleet was in action in the Baltic Sea. After being joined by the French fleet in August they attacked the Russian forts at Bomarsand, which surrendered without a fight. After leaving the Baltic for the winter, they returned the following year and bombarded Sveaborg (Viborg). In one of the minor raids along the coast Lieutenant Dowell won a Victoria Cross for towing a sinking cutter from under the Russian guns and rescuing the crew.

Bomb ketches with mortars manned by the RMA in the Baltic, 1855.

Marine battalions seized positions to open up the Sea of Azov in 1855 and in June the British and French assaulted Sevastopol. Severe damage was done to the embrasures and parapets of the guns thereby laying the crews open to heavy fire. During a sortie to patch up the damage Bombardier Thomas Wilkinson exposed himself to enemy fire in order to inspire his comrades to repair the shattered defences. This subsequently earned him the third Victoria Cross for the Royal Marines.

World-Wide Wars of the 19th Century: 1855–1873

It was also in 1855 that an Order in Council was issued designating the infantry a 'Light Corps', a title prized as an honour and the training being considered "the best adapted to the nature which the Corps is generally required to perform when employed ashore". The two Corps thus became the Royal Marine Artillery, the 'Blue Marines' and the Royal Marine Light Infantry, 'The Red Marines'. A recruit Depot opened at Deal, Kent in 1861.

In the Indian Mutiny, which broke out in 1857, RM detachments were landed from HM Ships and small parties of Marines were in action at Cawnpore and took part in the Relief of Lucknow. At the same time two battalions were formed in England and sent out to the Second China War and these were joined by a third Provisional Battalion, three hundred strong under Lieutenant Colonel Thomas Lemon, from India, where it had been garrisoning Calcutta. They occupied the vast city of Canton in January 1858, which had been the scene of a fierce battle by nearly two hundred Marines eighteen months earlier, when they fought to take the city forts one by one. In June 1857 Marines were involved in the Battle of Fatshan Creek and later the 1st and 2nd Marines, by now reinforced, attacked the Taku Forts which guarded the mouth of the Pei-ho river. The Marines landed in small boats and had to cross wide mud flats and water filled ditches before reaching the walls. The ranks were cut to ribbons and it is recorded that *"Not 150 men reached the second ditch, and only fifty the third, at the foot of the ramparts. A single scaling ladder was thrown up and a mere ten men tried to force the great fortress. They then withdrew with great difficulty"*. The Marines subsequently provided a guard for the naval contingent in Tientsin. When the Taku Forts were taken the following year, the Marines were once again to the fore. They were with the British 1st Division when it entered Peking in 1860. During the Second China War the Marines had lost 232 men killed and twenty-two wounded.

At the end of 1863, when there was internal strife in Japan, an RMLI Battalion went out to reinforce the Legation Guard at Yokohama where they had been threatened by the Samurai. To carry the battalion HMS *Conqueror* had been converted by the removal of her main deck guns, shades of the Commando ships a century later. The following year they formed part of an allied force that attacked Simonoseki, thus ending the anti-foreign movement in Western Japan.

A group of RMLI Officers at Forton Barracks, Gosport c.1867.

Another battalion went out to Yokohama in 1870 and remained there for five years, being well received not only by the Japanese people, but by the Mikado himself. A battalion serving in Mexico in 1861 even provided a mounted detachment and seven years later, Marines from HM Ships were landed with a naval brigade taking a modest part in the Abyssinian expedition.

This was now a time for imperial policing and a period during which the strength of the Corps remained fairly steady. Nevertheless, as an economy measure, after an existence of only fifty-six years, Woolwich Division was closed in 1869, when Officers were placed on half-pay and men forcibly discharged. However, in the same year the Depot at Deal was enlarged when North and South Barracks were taken over.

Troubles in Africa and the Far East: 1873–1898

Since the abolition of the slave trade in 1807, the security of British trading settlements on the coast of West Africa had been largely left to the Admiralty, which kept ships off the coast to suppress slavers and pirates. In 1873, when the Ashanti threatened the coast in West Africa, a small mixed contingent of RMA, with two mountain guns and two hundred war rockets, plus 110 RMLI, under Lieutenant Colonel Francis Festing RMA, was sent out in June to restore order.

Supported by Marines and seamen from the fleet they defeated two thousand Ashanti, but by the end of July most had gone down with fever and were replaced by two hundred Marines from the UK. Later in the year they joined up with a force of three Army battalions which, after some jungle skirmishes, forced the Ashanti back into their own territory. RM ships' detachments served ashore with naval brigades in Malaya in 1874/5, in Zanzibar in 1875, the Congo in 1875/6, in Samoa in 1876, on the Niger in 1876/7 and afloat in the constant task of defeating slavery. Cyprus was ceded to Britain in 1878 and seamen and Marines occupied the island until a permanent garrison arrived. In the following year Marines from the fleet formed part of the naval brigade during the Zulu War.

War broke out in Egypt in June 1882 when Britain supported the Khedive against the dictator Arabi Pasha; large numbers of the RMA and RMLI were soon involved. Unable to intervene to stop the rioting and murder of Europeans in Alexandria, the Mediterranean Fleet bombarded the batteries and when Arabi Pasha's Egyptian Army withdrew, ships' detachments were formed into a battalion and landed to hold the city and restore order. The arrival of the Channel Squadron in July with more Marines, joined in August by another mixed RMA/RMLI battalion, resulted in the seizure of Port Said and Ismailia almost without resistance. The Marines were later reorganised

The RMLI storming the lines at Tel-el-Kebir, 1882. *From a sketch by Colonel Field.*

25

into an RMA and an RMLI Battalion and, with the former serving as infantry, joined General Sir Garnet Wolseley's force preparing to march on Cairo from the Suez Canal, whilst Arabi's attention was fixed on Alexandria. The RMA Battalion soon saw action with an advance force under General Graham at Kassassin and after a night march both battalions were in the dawn attack on the strongly held fortified lines at Tel-el-Kebir, which covered the approaches to Cairo. With the RMLI Battalion being the first to storm the defences, a fierce battle resulted in RMLI losses of thirteen killed and fifty-four wounded, but the Egyptians were routed. The force reached Cairo the following day and on 19 October the two Marine battalions returned to England.

Having put the Khedive back on the throne, the British found themselves faced with the problem of the Sudan where the Mahdi had risen against Egyptian rule. Once more 150 seamen and Marines were hastily landed in February 1884, this time from ships at Suakin, before a battalion from the Mediterranean Fleet arrived, to be joined later by another battalion from the UK. They fought actions at El Teb on the Red Sea coast and at Tamai where Osman Digma's 'fuzzy-wuzzies' proved tenacious. At El Teb 380 Marines positioned on the left flank carried out a daring flanking movement against the Mahdi's men who were encamped in the hills. Thousands of Dervishes rose up and charged down the hill at the main square of troops, but they were cut down with a loss of three thousand of their six thousand men. An RMLI company served with the Guards Camel Regiment in the Desert Column in the attempt to relieve Khartoum. The fierce action at Abu Klea on 17 January 1885 was described by Winston Churchill as *the most savage action fought by the British troops in the Sudan*. During the re-conquest of the Sudan in 1896, RMA NCOs trained and supervised Egyptians manning guns in the river gunboats on the Nile, whilst Officers from both branches of the Corps were seconded to the Egyptian Army and saw action at the Battle of Omdurman.

An unusual occurrence during this period was the deployment of a detachment on Special Service to Dublin in 1882/3. After the infamous Phoenix Park murders when Lord Frederick Cavendish, the Chief Secretary of Ireland, and others were assassinated, three hundred specially selected Marines dressed in plain clothes spent six months on policing and guard duties in Ireland.

As this era drew to a close varying numbers of the Corps were in action on the Irrawaddy in Burma, in East and West Africa between 1891 and 1896, in Sierra Leone and Zanzibar in 1896 and even in Crete. During the 1890s Royal Marines battalions were formed each year to train with the Army at Aldershot and for several years battalions from Plymouth did so on Dartmoor – shades of things to come. As the pressures of sea service increased and the prospect of action ashore diminished, military training on this scale became subsidiary to the needs of the fleet.

Boers and Boxers: 1899–1902

When the Second Boer War broke out in South Africa in 1899 to meet the demands for field artillery, the Navy brought ships' guns ashore and mounted them on improvised carriages while the RM detachments provided the escorts. The British garrisons of Cape Colony and Natal found themselves heavily outnumbered and outgunned as the Boers had brought in heavy calibre weapons and the highly mobile Boer commandos proved more than a nuisance. However, the six-inch naval guns on their makeshift mountings proved more than a match for the Boers. On 25 November the RMLI had a chance to show their expertise as an assault force in the Battle of Graspan. After a preliminary bombardment they advanced in extended order across

The Battle of Graspan.
From a painting by Charles Stadden.

27

the open veldt under enemy fire. Their losses of eight killed and eighty-three wounded out of a total force of 190 Marines were severe as they were such an easy target in their tight formation only four paces apart. Over on the east coast another naval brigade was formed from ships at Durban and whilst the naval guns provided artillery support for the advance on Ladysmith the Marines were landed only to provide the infantry defence of the city.

At the end of May 1900, on the other side of the globe the Boxers were threatening the foreign legations in Peking. Included in the international force that was assembled, the RMLI provided three Officers and seventy-six Marines plus three naval ratings and the US Marine Corps two Officers and fifty-three men, the first time the two Corps had fought alongside each other. Besides the British and American legations, there were Russian, German, Italian, Austrian and Japanese missions contained within the small compound adjacent to the Imperial City walls. The force arrived on the 13th and a week later, the Imperial government ordered the legations to leave but, on his way to discuss evacuation, the German minister was murdered by his Chinese escort, and so the siege began. The Chinese established themselves close round the perimeter and made constant forays, burning buildings and shooting at anything that moved.

On 24 June Captain Lewis Halliday RMLI, with a section of twenty men, was severely wounded when leading a sortie against the Boxer intruders. Despite his wounds he engaged the enemy in hand to hand fighting eventually driving them off. For his gallantry he was awarded the Victoria Cross, whilst a CGM and five DCMs were awarded to RM NCOs of the Legation detachment. It was from operating so closely together during the fifty-five-day siege in Peking that today's strong bond between the Royal Marines and the United States Marine Corps was established.

The Corps also took a prominent part in the large international relief force which set out from the mouth of the Peiho River on 9 June. Travelling by rail towards Peking, they were brought to a halt twenty-five miles from the city where the rails had been torn up. After being attacked by Imperialist troops, they staged a withdrawal towards Tientsin. In the early hours of the 21st they came under heavy fire from the Hsuku arsenal, and Major Johnstone led his Marines and half a company of seamen back up the road, across the river and made a bayonet attack on the fortress, driving the Boxers out. This provided

Royal Marines manning the 'International' gun at Peking.

plenty of food and supplies for the beleaguered column. More heavy fighting broke out around Tientsin on 4 August but this was repulsed and the column eventually reached Peking on the 15th, much to the relief of the legation guards.

Chapter 4

Early Twentieth Century

1902–1939

Queen Victoria had appointed her second son, HRH The Prince Alfred, Duke of Edinburgh and Duke of Saxe Coburg-Gotha as Honorary Colonel of the Royal Marines in 1882. He died in 1900 and on 2 January 1901, HRH The Duke of York, the Prince of Wales' second son, became Colonel-in-Chief of the Royal Marine Forces, a revised title which was much favoured by the Corps and an appointment he continued to hold when he became King George V in 1910. In 1902, as Prince of Wales, he led a brigade of four Marine battalions past his father, King Edward VII, at the Aldershot coronation review. After Queen Victoria died at Osborne House on the Isle of Wight on 22 January 1901, Royal Marines bands played in the funeral procession, while RMLI sentries from Forton kept watch on the coffin as it lay overnight in the Royal Yacht *Victoria & Albert*. The following day Royal Marines from Forton were formed up as the funeral train steamed slowly past.

In 1903, the Royal Marines assumed responsibility for providing bands in

One of the last Royal Naval Bands – HMS *Calcutta*.

HM Ships and RN shore establishments, and the Royal Naval School of Music was formed at Eastney. Divisional bands had been established at Chatham, Portsmouth, and Plymouth with their own methods of entry, training and engagement, but ships' bands had always been formed partly by privately engaging musicians for the commission and partly from a small naval band service founded in 1863. Now they would have their own pay, conditions, training and promotion structure leading to commissioned rank as Musical Directors.

The Fisher Reforms of the early years of the century had a disastrous effect on the Corps when, with the naval vote increasing, their numbers were gradually reduced and those who served spent most of their time at sea. Admiral Sir John Fisher was well aware of the under-employment of RM Officers afloat, but as he hated the Army, the Navy's rival for public funds, he would not tolerate most RM Officers' desire for military training and even employment ashore. He even introduced a scheme whereby all Officers for the naval service carried out the same training and cadets appointed to the Marines were commissioned as Lieutenants (M). This was against strong opposition from the Corps and resulted in an acute shortage of junior Officers when war broke out in 1914. No doubt if Fisher had been asked 'What are the Marines for?' he would have replied that they were there to man the guns of the fleet. This held little truck with the seamen who were now a much more disciplined long-service body, and who excelled at naval gunnery themselves.

The Great War

On the outbreak of hostilities in 1914, the majority of the Corps was serving at sea, but a Royal Marine Brigade was immediately formed largely from reservists and partially trained recruits. The RMA, Chatham, Portsmouth and Plymouth Divisions each provided a battalion and in three weeks this formation was on the other side of the Channel. It was withdrawn after only seven days and the RMA battalion was relieved by one from Deal. It was now realised that Antwerp was the major threat and, after a visit from Winston Churchill, then First Lord of the Admiralty, the Marine Brigade was ordered there on 4 October, but not before two hundred men were despatched to Dunkirk to serve with the RN Air Service armoured cars, popularly known as 'The Motor Bandits'. The Brigade was subsequently joined by two naval brigades which had formed up at Walmer;

thus creating the nucleus of the famous RN Division. The Antwerp operation was a strategic success, allowing more time for the Army to extend its flank northwards. The Division was withdrawn to the UK and reorganised on Army lines, brought up to strength and prepared for service overseas.

On being withdrawn from the RM Brigade the RMA Battalion was formed into two artillery brigades for service in France, one of super heavy fifteen-inch howitzers on field mountings, the other of light AA pom-poms. By 1916 there were ten of these heavy howitzers in action and they supported most of the great offensives on the Western Front, playing a particularly important role on the Somme and at Passchendale. Their casualties in the latter action were thirty-five killed and ninety-seven wounded, in addition to the many who were badly gassed.

Royal Marine Artillery ashore in Belgium in 1914, still wearing blue uniforms.

Recruiting in 1793. *An engraving by Bunbury.*

The First Fleet nearing Australia in 1788. *From a painting by Rex Phillips.*

THE EARLY MARINE REGIMENTS 1664–1748

Left to Right: A Grenadier and Ensign with the Lieutenant Colonel's Colour, Duke of York and Albany's Maritime Regiment, 1664; Prince George of Denmark's Regiment, 1686; Earl of Torrington's Marines, 1691; Holt's Regiment of Marines; Earl of Donegal's Regiment for Sea Service; Fox's, Villier's and Saunderson's Marines, 1702–1712; 1st, 4th, 2nd and 6th Marines, 1740–1748; Private, Marine Invalid Company, 1749. *A painting by Charles Stadden in the RM Museum.*

THE MARINE CORPS AND THE ROYAL MARINES 1755–1807

Left to Right: Sergeant 1775, Drummer, 1758 and Officer with the Colour, 1760, The Marine Corps; Officer (Grenadier Company), 1773, Grenadier, 1775 and Sergeant (Grenadier Company), 1780, The Marine Corps; Surgeon, 1773, Private (Light Company), 1775, Grenadier, 1789 and Sergeant, 1790, The Marine Corps; Officer, 1795, Officer (in Greatcoat), 1798, The Marine Corps; Sergeant, 1805 and Drummer, 1807, Royal Marines. *A painting by Charles Stadden in the RM Museum.*

THE ROYAL MARINES AND THE ROYAL MARINE ARTILLERY 1807–1854

Left to Right: Two Privates RMA (Blue Undress and Full Dress), 1807; RM Officer, 1815; Gunner RMA, 1817; RM Officer (Full Dress), 1823; RM Private (Drill Order), 1830; Trumpeter RMA and Drummer RM, 1829; Two RM Officers (Undress Frock and Undress Afloat), c.1838; RM Bandsman, 1825; RMA Officer, 1848; RM Private (Marching Order) and Bombardier RMA (Undress), 1854. *A painting by Charles Stadden in the RM Museum.*

THE ROYAL MARINE ARTILLERY AND LIGHT INFANTRY 1854–1900

Left to Right: RM Private (Crimea), 1854; RMLI Private (China), 1859; Two RMA Officers (Mess Dress and Full Dress), c.1870; Two RMLI Privates (Ashanti War and Full Dress), c.1874; RMLI Officer (Service Dress, Egypt, 1882) and Corporal (Camel Regiment, Sudan 1885); RMA Boats Crew, RMA Gunner (Drill Order), Drummer (Undress), 1896; RMA Gunner (Greatcoat), Adjutant (Undress) and Bugler (Marching Order), 1900. *A painting by Charles Stadden in the RM Museum.*

THE ROYAL MARINE ARTILLERY AND LIGHT INFANTRY 1900–1923

Left to Right: RMA (Working Dress), 1916; RMLI Marching Order, 1900 and 1917; RMLI Officers (Mess Dress 1900 and Review Order 1908); RMA Musician, 1910; RMA Officers (Review Order 1900, Undress 1922 and Mess Dress 1900); RMLI Drummer (Review Order), 1904; RMLI Officer (Drill Order), 1904; RMA Field Officer (Drill Order), 1914; RMA Gunner (SW Africa), 1917; RMLI SNCO (Tropical), 1900. *A painting by Charles Stadden in the RM Museum.*

THE ROYAL MARINES 1923–1946

Left to Right: Colonel Commandant (Review Order), 1928; Field Officer (Mess Dress), 1939; Officer (Battle Dress), 1941; Marine (Embarkation Order), 1938; Marine (Khaki Drill), 1939; Colour Sergeant (Review Order), 1935; RM Commando, 1944; QMSI (Drill Order), 1939; Khaki (Drill Order), 1939; Corporal (Provost Company), 1943; Marine (Blue Battledress), 1944; RM Commando (Far East), 1945; Divisional Band and General Officer, Review Order, 1938. *A painting by Charles Stadden in the RM Museum.*

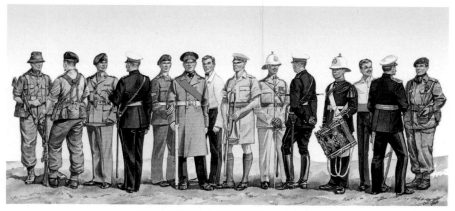

THE ROYAL MARINES 1946–1973

Left to Right: Marine (Malaya), 1951; Corporal (Southern Arabia), 1964; Officer (Khaki Service Dress), 1946; RSM (No 1 Dress), 1969; Corporal (Lovat Dress), 1969; Colour Sergeant (Greatcoat), 1948; SNCO (Tropical Mess Dress), 1959; Musician (Tropical Dress), 1959; Officer (Khaki Drill), 1960; Adjutant (Blue Uniform), 1956; Bugler (Ceremonial), 1969; Officer (Red Sea Rig), 1959; General Officer (Ceremonial), 1964; Marine (Combat Dress), 1969. *A painting by Charles Stadden in the RM Museum.*

THE ROYAL MARINES AND THE CORPS FAMILY 1972-2014

Left to Right: CSgt Bugler 1972; Sgt 42 Cdo, Northern Ireland 1972; Mne UN Service 1975; WO1 Lovat uniform 1980; Mne Falklands 1982; Cpl, on Exercise in Belize 1990; Marine Gulf War 1991; Lt 45 Cdo Southern Turkey 1991; RMPT Fleet Protection Gp RM North Arabian Gulf 2003; Maj RMR; Mountain Leader Norway; Mne 45 Cdo Helmand Afghanistan 2009; Musn RMA Concert Band; Cpl SBS 2014; RM Cadet; Mne, multi terrain pattern uniform 2013; Mne, Remembrance Sunday 2011. *A painting by William Webb in the RM Museum.*

The Cutting Out of 'La Chevrette', 1801.
From a painting in Bristol City Art Gallery by de Loutherberg.

While inspecting the guard aboard Bellerophon, Napoleon remarked that much might be done with 100,000 men such as these! *From a painting by Captain Hicks.*

The Battle of Hernani during the Carlist War, 1837.
From a painting by Cunliffe.

A Royal Marine Artillery field battery on Southsea Common, c.1843.
From a painting by Cunliffe.

The RMLI provided a Company for the Guards Camel Regiment.
'A Halt in the Bayuda Desert', 1885. *From a painting by Bartelli.*

Royal Marines landing from HMS *Vindictive* at Zeebrugge, 1918.
From a painting by de Lacy.

Gallipoli

In January 1915, when Turkey entered the war on the side of the Central Powers, a decision was made to open up the Dardanelles by a naval attack. After the first bombardments protection for naval demolition parties was provided by RM detachments landed from two of the bombarding battleships. The first elements of the RM Brigade, the Chatham and Plymouth Battalions had already sailed for the Eastern Mediterranean in February. The first to land were two companies of the Plymouth Battalion, also as protection for demolition parties, one company went ashore at Sedd-el-Bahr and the other at Kum Kale on the other side of the Dardanelles, thereby operating against the Turks on two continents simultaneously. Their tasks mainly accomplished after meeting strong opposition, they were able to re-embark in good order. The main contribution from the Corps came later in the form of the Royal Naval Division under the command of an RMA General, (later Sir) Archibald Paris, which, with the 29th Division, landed on the southernmost tip of the Gallipoli Peninsula. The Corps provided No 3 Brigade with the Chatham, Portsmouth and Plymouth Battalions, while the Deal Battalion was in No 1 Brigade, commanded by Brigadier General D Mercer with the Drake and Nelson Battalions of seamen.

On 25 April Plymouth Battalion RMLI landed on 'Y' Beach on the left flank, were in action for thirty hours and took heavy casualties from a Turkish counter-attack.

The Gallipoli Beaches, 1915.

Three days later the Chatham and Portsmouth Battalions landed at Anzac beach and took over the centre of the line, being joined two days later by Deal and Nelson battalions. It was during the fierce fighting here that Lance Corporal W R Parker, a stretcher-bearer, was taking supplies to forward positions across open ground which was being swept by machine gun fire. Despite most of his companions being killed, he pressed on and assisted the wounded in the forward trenches to safety. For this selfless action he was awarded the VC. As the campaign developed into a stalemate the freezing blizzards, severe frostbite and flooded trenches during the winter took their toll and casualties mounted. The losses in the four Marine Battalions were so great that the remnants of Chatham and Deal were amalgamated into the 1st Battalion RMLI and those of Portsmouth and Plymouth into the 2nd RMLI. Troops were gradually withdrawn and the 2nd Battalion were the final troops to leave giving rise to the maxim 'First in, last out'. The RM casualties at Gallipoli were over one hundred Officers and three thousand NCOs and men killed or wounded.

The Western Front

From Gallipoli the Division moved to the Western Front and arriving in France it was re-equipped and reorganised. Together with the Howe and Anson Naval Battalions, the two RMLI Battalions formed the 188th Infantry Brigade of the renamed 63rd (Royal Naval) Division. In addition to the two battalions, the Corps provided the Divisional Machine Gun Battalion and RMLI Officers commanded some of the naval battalions, whilst others were company commanders.

At Passchendale, on one day, the RMLI lost 680 men killed, wounded or missing out of a total of 1,170. The action in and around the village of Gavrelle in the closing stages of the Battle of Arras in April 1917 saw the highest number of Royal Marine casualties in a single day in the Corps' history - on 28 April the RN Division's 1st and 2nd RMLI battalions suffered 846 killed, missing or wounded. The 1st Battalion was effectively wiped out when it charged a German strongpoint north of the village, found the barbed wire still intact and was enfiladed, while the 2nd battalion suffered almost as badly in the fighting around the windmill that formed part of the German line to the north-east. By 1918 their losses were so severe that the battalions were reduced

A fifteen-inch Howitzer of the RMA in action on the Western Front, 1917.

to one and the 1st Battalion RMLI ended the war in the pursuit to Mons. The Royal Marine Artillery, providing a Howitzer Brigade and an AA Brigade, were engaged in almost every action on the Western Front from Aubers in 1915 onwards, including the Somme, Ancre, Ypres, Passchendale, Cambrai, Arras and many others.

The fighting done by a tiny minority of the Corps, to whit the RMLI Battalions and the RMA on the Western Front, was far more than the rest of the Royal Marines in the whole war. The only Victoria Cross awarded to the Corps on the Western Front was to Major F W Lumsden RMA, whilst commanding an Army battalion in France in 1917. He was killed a year later in the front line when commanding a Brigade soon after adding a third bar to the DSOs he had won in 1917. He was also appointed CB in the King's Birthday Honours for 1918. A memorial to him stands in the Royal Marines Museum Garden of Remembrance at Eastney.

At sea the Marines were also engaging the Germans. On 31 May 1916, some 132 Officers and Warrant Officers and 5,700 NCOs and men were present at the major naval engagement of the war, the Battle of Jutland. Manning turrets in most of the capital ships they kept the guns firing. In the battle cruiser HMS *Lion*, flagship of Admiral Beatty, an eleven-inch shell hit 'Q' turret, manned by Marines, blowing open the roof and killing most of the gun's crew. Major Harvey RMLI, having lost both legs, gave the order to flood the magazine thus ensuring that the fire did not spread below to the magazine and blow up the ship. He was awarded a posthumous Victoria Cross, but fifty Royal Marines in the ship were killed in the action. However the highest proportion of Royal Marines decorated from one ship at Jutland was to HMS *Chester*, where the OCRM Captain Edward Bamford was awarded the DSO and five of his forty Marines were also rewarded. This was the single most bloody day in the history of the Corps with 526 men killed on a single day.

Zeebrugge

"I am confident that the great traditions of our forefathers will be worthily maintained, and that all ranks will strive to emulate the heroic deeds of our brothers in France and Flanders" concluded the message Vice Admiral Roger Keyes sent to the Officers and men taking part in the gallant raid on Zeebrugge in 1918. The task was to stop the U-boats that were based on the Bruges canals from putting to sea. The 4th Battalion Royal Marines, quickly reorganised in Deal with a cover story that they were training for a raid in France with the Royal Naval Division. After a fortnight's training and waiting for the right conditions, the force sailed on the moonlit night of 22 April. As it left, Keyes signalled *"St George for England"* to which Captain Carpenter in HMS *Vindictive* replied *"May we give the dragon's tail a damned good twist!"*

The plan was to block the canal entrances with three obsolete cruisers and the job of the *Vindictive*, along with the requisitioned Liverpool ferryboats *Iris* and *Daffodil*, was to carry the storming parties. Marines and sailors under Lieutenant Colonel Elliot and Captain Halahan RN were to silence the gun batteries on the Zeebrugge mole that protected the harbour while the blockships were scuttled. The approach was made under cover of drizzle and an elaborate smoke screen, but a sudden breeze blew the smoke away when the *Vindictive* was about four hundred yards off and the attackers were met with the full force of the enemy guns on the mole. Elliot and Halahan were both killed but the attack went in with the troops storming across the remaining two specially constructed wooden brows

The brows aboard Vindictive, constructed for landing on the Zeebrugge Mole.

or gangplanks. They berthed three hundred yards further on from their planned position and then had to drop down sixteen feet from the top of the wall to the main level of the mole, all under heavy fire. The German guns were particularly aimed at the foretop positions in the ship where Marines were manning the guns. Sergeant N A Finch RMA was one of these and despite all around him being killed or wounded, he continued to work his Lewis gun. Meanwhile Capt E Bamford RMLI, who had already won a DSO in HMS *Chester* at the Battle of Jutland, led Portsmouth Company along the mole *"displaying the greatest initiative in the command of his company and a complete disregard of danger"* and took the German strong point before assaulting the battery. After an hour the remnants of the attackers, taking their wounded with them, re-embarked and returned to England. Two Victoria Crosses were awarded to the 4th Battalion to be balloted for under the 9th Statute of the Order and these went to Bamford and Finch. As a mark of respect it was decreed that no future RM battalion would ever be numbered 4th.

When he visited the 4th Battalion at Deal on 7 March 1918 before they sailed for Zeebrugge, King George V also witnessed recruit training. He decreed that the senior recruit squad under training should henceforth be known as the King's Squad and the best all-round recruit should be awarded the King's Badge, providing he reached a sufficiently high standard (*see Appendix G*).

Other World War 1 Activities

Royal Marine Engineers, specially raised for the war, constructed camps and installations for the Royal Navy and towards the end of hostilities there was even an RM Labour Corps working the Channel Ports. In South Africa in 1916 Royal Marines trained members of the Union Defence Force and subsequently fought through the East African campaigns of 1916 and 1917.

Russia 1918–1919 and Expeditions to Ireland and Chanak

An ad hoc Royal Marines Field Force had been sent to Murmansk in July 1918 and was deployed along the three hundred miles of railway from there to Kem on the White Sea. Further east in 1919, thirty Royal Marines volunteers and some sailors, under the command of Captain Thomas Jameson, from HMS *Suffolk* and *Kent* travelled six thousand miles from Vladivostock across Siberia to support the Russian White Army. After transporting one six-inch gun and four twelve-pounder guns on

Royal Marines with the six-inch gun they transported by rail across Siberia in 1919.

railway trucks, they mounted the large gun on to a paddle driven tug and took part in operations on the Kama River, a tributary of the Volga.

The Field Force was relieved by the 6th Battalion and this proved an unhappy time when the greater part of two companies mutinied. After a court martial one Officer was dismissed the Service while one NCO and twelve men were sentenced to death for 'wilful defiance', which was later commuted to five years penal servitude, while seventy-six men were sentenced to various other punishments.

The 8th Battalion spent two years in Southern Ireland arriving there in June 1920 to guard coastal installations during early Sinn Fein troubles. There was a happier outcome to the 11th Battalion's tour to Constantinople where they arrived on 2 October 1922 deploying alongside the Army, all protecting the city and covering the Chanak bridgehead, which held open the Dardanelles' sea route. They withdrew after a year.

Amalgamation in 1923

The amalgamation of the Royal Marine Artillery and the Royal Marine Light Infantry into a single Corps had been under consideration since the end of the Great War, when demobilisation reduced the Corps strength from 55,000 to 15,000. By 1922, the Treasury, after trying to abolish the Royal Marines, reduced their number to 9,500 on the understanding that one Division was given up. Forton Barracks at Gosport was closed and Eastney Barracks, completed in 1864 to house the RMA, was retained to become the home of the Portsmouth Division Royal Marines.

The amalgamation decision was announced by an Admiralty Fleet Order of June 1923 and the ranks of Gunner and Private were replaced by that of Marine. A cadre of Officers and NCOs would continue to be trained at the School of Land Artillery in Fort Cumberland, but otherwise the training of the Corps would be as infantrymen and seaman gunners, with Deal chosen as the centralised recruit training establishment. The Corps needed a new role and the official instructions read:

> Its function in war and peace is to provide detachments which, whilst fully capable of manning their share of the gun armament of ships, are specially trained to provide a striking force, drawn either from the Divisions or from the Fleet, immediately available for use under the direction of the Commander-in-Chief for amphibious operations such as raids on the enemy coastline and bases, or the seizure and defence of temporary bases for the use of our own Fleet.

In January 1927, when the Chinese Nationalist armies were marching on Shanghai, the 12th Battalion was hastily formed and sailed within a week. They formed part of the Shanghai Defence Force to guard the international settlements, and when the tension eased in December, they were withdrawn to England.

In 1935, Italy invaded Abyssinia and in view of the threat of war, 1,600 Marines were sent out to Egypt to set up defences at Alexandria, where they provided coast artillery as well as manning anti-aircraft guns and searchlights. All the men returned to the UK in July 1936. This was the forerunner of the two Mobile Naval Base Defence Organisations (MNBDO) that were subsequently raised with a huge investment in men and equipment for the forthcoming war. On return to England a nucleus was retained at Fort Cumberland where pier-building equipment and the Landing Craft Mechanized were developed. Although the amphibious concept might seem to be taking shape it still lagged badly, not least in the Admiralty, where in 1938 the First Sea Lord said that he did not foresee a combined operation being mounted in the next war! The Americans had a different view and were well ahead of Britain in amphibious matters when war broke out.

Ranks of the 12th RM Battalion embarking for service in Shanghai, 1927.

The early days of landing craft in Langstone Harbour Portsmouth, 1929.

Also in 1935, Silver Jubilee year, the Royal Marines carried out ceremonial duties in London for the first time, when a specially formed battalion mounted guard on Buckingham Palace, St James's and on other places of note. Before leaving London, they were able to exercise the privilege of marching through the City with bayonets fixed, drums beating and Colours flying for the first time.

Transport being landed from one of HM ships during an exercise in the 1930s.

49

An RM Battalion carried out ceremonial duties in London for the first time in 1935.

The only visit King Edward VIII paid to the Corps during his short reign was to Eastney in 1936, with Commander Lord Louis Mountbatten as his ADC.

They also participated in the other Jubilee ceremonies and two years later in the Coronation of King George VI, keeping the Corps in the public eye at a time when morale was suffering.

Before World War One eleven Royal Marines Officers, one sergeant RMA and one private RMLI were among the first pilots to be trained for the Royal Naval Air Service. Notably, in 1911 Lieutenant E L Gerrard RMLI was one of the first four naval pilots and the following year Private J Edmonds was the third Royal Marine to qualify. During the Great War twenty-two Royal Marines or former Royal Marines pilots and seventeen observers flew with the RNAS and RFC. Later, from 1924 Royal Marines were once again called to volunteer for flying duties and thirty seven officers flew with the Fleet Air Arm during the 1920s and 1930s prior to the Second World War.

A flight of aircraft from HMS *Glorious*, all with RM pilots, over Malta in 1931.

Chapter 5

The Second World War
1939–1945

In 1939 most of the Corps were once again serving at sea when war with Germany broke out. The strength of the Royal Marines was 12,390 with a further 1,082 in the Royal Fleet Reserve. A skeleton organisation was already in being to provide defences for naval bases and this was expanded with reservists and conscripts providing most of the men. From this the RM Fortress Unit was quickly mobilised and sent to Scapa Flow. RM Engineers were formed again and carried out construction work in naval shore establishments and a Siege Regiment, equipped with fourteen-inch and 13.5-inch guns, was formed to bombard the French coast from railway sidings around the Dover area. By the end of the year, Royal Marines had also been in action at sea, particularly in the Battle of the River Plate.

When the Germans invaded Norway in April 1940 some of the first ashore were Marines from HMS *Glasgow* and *Sheffield*, landing at Namsos and working

Named after Sir Winston Churchill, the RM Siege Regiment's fourteen-inch gun 'Winnie', firing from St Margaret's Bay, Kent, 1940.

with the Norwegian Army. Marines from HMS *Nelson, Hood* and *Barham* followed, landing at Åndalsnes and Ålesund to set up coastal defences while the Fortress Unit went to Northern Norway. Some small ad hoc parties were sent across the Channel, covering the departure of the Queen of the Netherlands from the Hook of Holland and the final withdrawal from Boulogne and Calais. Elements of MNBDO1 were widely deployed along the south east coast during the Battle of Britain and the 1st Heavy Anti-Aircraft Regiment registered a record score, accounting for ninety-eight enemy aircraft.

In August the newly formed RM Brigade was despatched to Dakar in an ill-fated operation aimed at persuading the Vichy French to join the Allies but it never landed. Shortly after returning it provided the basis on which a Royal Marine Division was assembled. Although the formation was chosen for a number of operations these never materialized.

The RM Band playing on the fo'c's'le of HMS *Rodney* at Scapa Flow in the Second World War.

During 1941 Marines were constantly in action at sea, on convoy work, in the battles of Crete and Cape Matapan and in the *Bismarck* action where the whole detachment of 164 Marines, including the band were lost when HMS *Hood* was sunk. The focus of the war then shifted to the Mediterranean and in January 1941 it was decided to send the MNBDO to the Middle East. After a journey

The MLC 'under sail' in which Major Ralph Garrett and his crew escaped from Crete in 1941.
From a painting by Rowland Langmaid.

around the Cape and through the Suez Canal, the formation was ordered to Crete but only about half reached the island a few days before the evacuation of Greece began in April. Defences were set up, but when German paratroops landed on 20 May, the Marines, fighting as infantry, were embroiled in the bloody battle and subsequent withdrawal. More than 1,200 Marines were taken prisoner but Major Ralph Garrett and 137 volunteers from the Marines and the Army refloated a derelict landing craft and, under improvised sail, managed to reach Egypt. A second MNBDO was raised in England.

Refitted after Crete MNBDO1 redeployed eastwards in September and set up their guns in Diego Garcia, the Seychelles and at Addu Atoll in the Indian Ocean. When war with Japan broke out in December 1941, one of the first actions was the sinking of HMS *Prince of Wales* and *Repulse*. A large proportion of the crews survived and Marines from the detachments joined up with the 2nd Battalion Argyll & Sutherland Highlanders, who had been reduced to 250 men after the fighting in Malaya. Together they formed a battalion and fought in the final stages before the fall of Singapore, inevitably as both ships were from Plymouth, as 'the Plymouth Argylls'. Those who survived were forced to surrender and spent the remainder of the war as prisoners of the Japanese. A further forty members of the RM detachments died as a result of the privations they endured working on the infamous 'railway of death'.

A pier constructed by Royal Marines to enable stores to be landed for the defence of the Seychelles, 1942.

Early in 1942 four Officers and 103 volunteers from the Coast Regiment of MNBDO1 went to Rangoon. As Force 'Viper' they were the last to leave the city and, manning motor launches were involved in heavy fighting, whilst covering the withdrawal up the River Irrawaddy. They finally abandoned and destroyed their craft before marching over the mountains into India. In Colombo and Trincomalee the Air Defence Brigade of MNBDO1 were in action when aircraft from the Japanese Fleet attacked Ceylon, while further south Major General Sturges with a skeleton HQ from the RM Division and two Army brigades seized Diego Suarez on Madagascar. When one of the Brigades was held up on the approaches to Antsirane, the RM Detachment of HMS *Ramillies* landed from a destroyer and captured the town.

Birth of Commandos

Winston Churchill had ordered the establishment of raiding forces soon after the fall of France and the Army formed their first Commando in the summer

Motor launches manned by Force Viper for operations on the Irrawaddy in Burma, 1942.

of 1940. The first Royal Marine Commando was formed in 1942 as The Royal Marine Commando and took part in the abortive Dieppe raid on 19 August that year. It became 'A' RM Commando later in the year when 'B' Commando was formed from the 8th Battalion in October. Nevertheless, there was some concerted feeling in the higher echelons of the Corps that the RM Division should still be retained, but it soon became apparent that the battalions were not being fully employed and the commando role was exactly what the Corps was all about.

Although the MNBDO cadre had been the first to develop landing craft before the war, little was done in the intervening years. The Admiralty now had an urgent need to man the large number of landing craft that would be required for the assault on mainland Europe. The appointment of Admiral Lord Mountbatten as Chief of Combined Operations, with his foresight and initiative, suggested that, together with the formation of Commandos, these were prime roles for the Royal Marines. With the help of a number of particularly influential leaders, he was able to bring about a reorganisation that changed the face of the Corps.

By January 1943 only one of the three major land formations in which the Corps were involved had seen any action and so the two MNBDOs returned to UK and disbanded. Although the AA regiments were retained and formed into

A Landing Craft Gun (Large) with its two 4.7-inch guns supporting partisans
in the Adriatic, 1945

an AA Brigade, most of the remaining ranks were re-trained for service with
Combined Operations. The RM Division was also disbanded, and the battalions
re-trained at Achnacarry for the commando role. Some of the remaining units
were reformed into specialist units in which Royal Marines personnel were
particularly suited and others were disbanded and the men also retrained for
service with Combined Operations. The Corps was now being prepared for
numerous active service roles in the invasion of Europe.

A new secret organisation with the misleading title of Royal Marine Boom
Patrol Detachment had been formed at Eastney. In December 1942 Major
'Blondie' Hasler led a team of twelve canoeists to place limpet mines on German
blockade runners lying up the Gironde river at Bordeaux. Five canoes, ten men,
were launched by submarine and only one crew, Hasler and Marine Sparks,
eventually escaped, the remainder being either killed during the raid or executed
by the Germans under Hitler's orders. This was the forerunner of the present
Special Boat Service, although the Army had started such an organisation earlier
in the war in the Mediterranean, which had included a few Marines.

Royal Marines Aviators

In the air, twenty-seven Royal Marines pilots and two observers saw action with the Fleet Air Arm in The Second World War and approximately eighty NCOs transferred to the Navy as rating pilots. They flew from aircraft carriers in all theatres of the war; in the Norwegian campaign, the Battle of Britain, at Matapan, Taranto and in support of the Sicily and Salerno landings, on D-Day and in the Pacific. Six DSOs, one OBE, one MBE, eight DSCs, six MIDs and four Battle of Britain Clasps were awarded to RM pilots for their bravery and many distinguished themselves in command appointments. Eighteen officers eventually commanded squadrons and eight became Commanders (Flying) culminating in 1945 when Lieutenant Colonel Ronnie Hay became the Air Group Co-ordinator commanding all 218 carrier-borne aircraft in the British Pacific Fleet.

The Mediterranean

As more Marines were trained the Royal Marines Commandos increased and they were numbered from 40 to 48(RM) Commandos, whilst the Army had Nos 1 to 12 Commandos. 40 & 41 Commandos took part on the left flank of the allied landings in Sicily on 10 July 1943 and in the assault on Salerno on 9 September. 41 Commando was involved in seizing the Vietri Pass leading towards Naples. 40 Commando took Termoli on 2 October, opening up the road north and then went into the line on the Garigliano. On 20 January 1944, 43 Commando landed on the Anzio beachhead where the Germans put up very strong resistance

In March a depleted 40 Commando and later 43 Commando were withdrawn from Italy and joined HQ 2 Special Service Brigade on the island of Vis in the Adriatic. Here they supported Tito's partisans in raids along the Yugoslav coast. A year later 43 Commando returned to the Italian mainland and it was on 3 April 1945 that Corporal Tom Hunter posthumously won the Corps' only Victoria Cross of The Second World War, leading a determined assault on an enemy position near Lake Comacchio.

North-West Europe

In Operation OVERLORD, the invasion of the Continent on 6 June 1944, the

Royal Marines made their greatest single contribution to the Second World War. In all some 17,500 Marines took part in the landings with four RM Commandos involved in the initial assault 41, 45, 47, 48, and with 46 Commando landing on D+1. 47 Commando's action to capture Port-en-Bessin on D+1 after a ten mile march beyond our own lines and replacing many of their weapons lost in the sea with German ones, was amongst the fiercest. Royal Marines also manned Centaur tanks in an Armoured Support Group of two regiments, which covered the initial landings. At sea the Corps manned two thirds of the assault landing craft, as well as serving in naval beach parties and obstruction clearance units. Nearly all the bombarding ships had Marines manning part of the main and secondary armament.

All five Commandos then took part in subsequent operations through France, Belgium and Holland. On 1st November 41, 47 & 48 Commandos landed at Westkapelle on the tip of Walcheren in the drive to secure the Scheldt with minor landing craft crewed by Royal Marines and manning the guns in the craft

The RM Armoured Support Group manned
Centaur Tanks for close support in Normandy, 1944.

47(RM) Commando embarking in LCTs for the Assault on Walcheren, 1944.

Commandos in the rubble of Wesel after crossing the Rhine, 1945.

of the Support Squadron. The support craft drew the fire of the German shore batteries from the assault craft and consequently suffered very heavy casualties.

During 1st SS Brigade's drive across Europe, 45 Commando was involved in a bitter battle at Montforterbeek on 23 January 1945 where Lance Corporal Harden RAMC, one of the unit's medical orderlies, won the VC. 45 & 46 Commandos were both involved in crossing the Rhine, Weser, Aller and Elbe rivers, finishing the war at Lubeck on the Baltic coast.. The 5th RM AA Brigade was responsible for the air defence of the port of Antwerp. To meet the Army's infantry shortage, two RM infantry brigades were formed in UK from landing craft crews, now surplus to requirements and in February 116 Brigade crossed the River Maas to enter Germany. 117 Brigade did not arrive in Europe until after VE Day and was only involved in the surrender of the German ports.

The Far East

Out in the Far East Marines from the East Indies Fleet seized the island of Cheduba in Burma in January 1944 and 3 SS Brigade, with 5 and 44 Commandos took part in the Arakan campaign in March. They were later joined by Nos 1 and 42 Commandos and then in January 1945, when the Japanese were in full retreat, the Brigade, now redesignated 3rd Commando Brigade and under the command of Brig C R Hardy, was sent to cut their escape route. 42 and 44 Commandos were involved in heavy fighting in the mangrove swamps around Kangaw. Having seized hill positions they were subjected to continuous artillery fire. In spite of their heavy casualties, for thirty-six hours the Commandos beat off the repeated counter attacks of the fanatical Japanese until the latter finally withdrew. In a Special Order of the Day General Sir Philip Christianson wrote *"the Battle of Kangaw has been the decisive battle of the whole Arakan campaign".*

As the war in the Far East ended in August 1945, Royal Marines were preparing for the invasion of Malaya, Operation ZIPPER, both as Commandos and landing craft crews. Force ROMA was hastily formed from Marines of the Far East Fleet to take the surrender in Penang, while 3 Commando Brigade was diverted to Hong Kong where it arrived in early September to assist in the liberation of the Colony. An Amphibian Support Regiment equipped with tracked amphibious vehicles had been formed in the UK to provide close support in the landings envisaged in operations along the coasts of Malaya, Indo-China and Thailand. It arrived in India shortly before VJ Day and was soon carrying out internal security duties as infantry in India and the Dutch East Indies.

By the end of the war the strength of the Corps had reached over 74,000. 3,983 Royal Marines had died during the war, including 225 musicians, a quarter of their strength, and the highest percentage of any branch of any Service. There was a reduction to peace-time strength, the principal roles of the Royal Marines changed and with that came a major reorganisation.

Force ROMA, hastily formed from RM detachments of the East Indies Fleet, land in Penang to take the Japanese surrender, 1945.

Chapter 6

Reorganisation and Deployments

1945–1951

Within two years of the end of the Second World War the numbers had reduced to 13,000 of whom 2,200 were in 3 Commando Brigade in the Far East and less than two thousand in the traditional pre-war role at sea. The functions of the Royal Marines now changed with the Corps becoming the leader in many aspects of amphibious warfare and exclusively assuming the Commando role, whilst still providing detachments and bands for HM Ships, albeit a dwindling task.

As regulars replaced 'hostilities only' men in commandos, the numerical designations of the Commandos were chosen to represent the three theatres of

Above The Commando Memorial above
Spean Bridge, unveiled in 1952.
Left The RM Commando Memorial,
Lympstone, unveiled in 1986.

war in which they had fought. 40 Commando was disbanded in the UK, but 44 Commando was renumbered '40' and represented the Mediterranean theatre, 42 Commando the Far East and 45 Commando North-West Europe.

The Harwell Committee, set up to examine the structure of the peace time services, recommended the abolition of the Corps, but fortunately the Admiralty did not agree although they insisted that the strength should be proportionate to that of the Royal Navy at ten percent. At the top General Sir Thomas Hunton changed his title, first to General Officer Commanding Royal Marines and then to Commandant General Royal Marines with direct access to the Admiralty Board. The Corps was streamlined in the next few years with the administrative Divisions becoming functional Groups; centralised pay, records and drafting; the formation of the RM Commando School, firstly at Towyn in North Wales and then Bickleigh in 1947; the Depot at Exton became the Infantry Training Centre; and the Royal Marine Forces Volunteer Reserve (now the Royal Marines Reserve), similar to the Territorial Army, initially of two hundred Officers and 1,300 other ranks was formed in 1948.

In order to achieve the reduction in the strength of the Corps, pressure was exerted on the Commandant General to disband the Commando Brigade, but in 1950 General Sir Leslie Hollis persuaded the Board of Admiralty that this could be accomplished by closing Chatham Group. In the summer of that year the massed bands of the Royal Marines Beat Retreat on Horse Guards Parade in London for the first time, an event which was later to be repeated at regular intervals in the ceremonial calendar of the Corps. This came to be seen as a precursor to the amalgamation of the bands formed from the Royal Naval School of Music and the old Divisional bands, to form the Royal Marines Band Service based on the Royal Marines School of Music at Deal later in the year and the appointment of its first Principal Director of Music, Lieutenant Colonel F Vivian Dunn.

By 1950 the Special Boat Company (later Squadron, and now Service) had become an all Royal Marines unit of a headquarters and six sections (one at Eastney, two in the Rhine Squadron, one with 3 Commando Brigade and two from the RMFVR), emanating from a variety of amphibious special forces units formed during the war.

So the Corps began to take on a new shape. Operationally it was fully employed with 3 Commando Brigade moving from Hong Kong to Malta in 1946. 40 Commando was soon involved in the Israeli/Palestinian unrest and two years later with 42 and 45 Commandos in the withdrawal from Palestine, 40 Commando being the last to leave. All three Commandos spent time in Egypt guarding lines of communications in the Canal Zone including the security of the Suez Canal. 45 Commando was sent to Akaba in Transjordan in 1949 when trouble threatened. One Commando was usually stationed in Cyprus. There is little doubt that the continued deployments of the Commando Brigade in keeping the peace around the world during this time helped the Admiralty change its mind about abolishing it. For the first time it became an affordable asset to the Senior Service.

Meanwhile at home His Majesty King George VI, who had succeeded to the title of Colonel-in-Chief on coming to the throne in 1937, changed his title to Captain General and soon afterwards dined with more than three hundred Royal Marines Officers at the Savoy Hotel in London on 21 December 1949.

Far East Unrest

In July 1949, Communist China threatened the sovereignty of Hong Kong, by massing on its border. 3 Commando Brigade was sent there, sailing together in the SS Georgic, with HQ, 40 & 42 Commandos embarking in Malta and picking up 45 Commando from Port Suez. For the next eight months they provided the internal security for Hong Kong and the hundreds of outlying islands.

In May 1950 the whole Brigade left Hong Kong for a tour of duty in the long drawn out Malayan Emergency. This was probably the most critical period of the whole campaign when violence reached its peak. The Chinese Communists, from bases deep in the jungle, were engaged in infiltrating Chinese and Malay villages, in terrorising the locals, arson, murder and other anti-colonial activities in an attempt to win over the hearts and minds of the people. 3 Commando Brigade was tasked with counter-insurgency warfare in support of the civil administration and police. In the northern state of Perak, the Brigade had responsibility for an area the size of Wales. The Headquarters and 42 Commando were initially based in Ipoh; 40 Commando in Taiping were given the Thailand border areas of Grik and Kroh; 45 Commando had an equally vast area centred on Tapah from the Cameron Highlands in the east to the coastal plain in the

A jungle patrol of 45 Commando searching a swamp for terrorists during the
Malayan Emergency, 1952.

west. In the next two years all three units were continually involved in jungle
fighting and counter terrorist activity. During this time they killed 171 terrorists
and captured more than fifty. The Commander-in-Chief, General Sir John
Harding, later described it as *"a record of hard work, devotion to duty and good
comradeship of which the Royal Marines have every reason to be proud"*. The Corps
lost thirty killed in the campaign and won forty gallantry awards, not including
'mentions in despatches'.

Meanwhile North Korean troops had crossed the 38th parallel into South
Korea on 25 June 1950 and a United Nations force was raised. In August a small
force of volunteers from the British Far East Fleet was placed at the disposal
of the US Navy to raid coastal communications, and the following month the
Commandant General was tasked with raising a special unit for this purpose. In
early September, 41 Independent Commando, some two hundred strong (later
three hundred), left UK for Japan under Lieutenant Colonel Douglas Drysdale.
They made three successful raids behind enemy lines cutting railway lines along
the north-eastern coast of Korea. In October 1950 The American and South
Korean forces followed up a defeated North Korean enemy across the border and
continued north beyond the port of Hungnam. When the Chinese attacked

A Bazooka team of 41 Commando. Issued with US weapons, equipment, and uniforms in Korea, 1952, they retained their green berets.

this force and cut the supply route between the Chosin Reservoir and Hungnam, 41 Commando were sent to join the 1st US Marine Division who were cut off at Hagaru-Ri, south of Chosin. The Commando, with trucks of supplies, together with a USMC infantry company and tanks, battled its way through mountainous country to join the garrison there against heavy opposition – losing a quarter of its strength - in atrocious arctic conditions. 41 then fought as part of the Marine Division in the subsequent withdrawal to the coast. After regrouping and retraining in Japan, 41 Commando landed on the north-eastern coast, 150 miles behind enemy lines on 7 April 1951. They remained ashore eight hours to demolish the railway line. In July they established a base on Wonsan Island sixty miles inside enemy territory from where they made a number of raids.

The unit was recalled to England at the end of 1951 being disbanded the following February. They had lost thirty-one killed including three RN medical staff while twenty-nine were taken prisoner, ten of whom died in captivity. Eighteen Officers and men were decorated apart from ten 'mentions' and thirteen US awards. For their part in the epic breakout at Hagaru-Ri, 41 Commando was subsequently awarded the high honour of a Presidential Unit Citation, which was later borne on their Regimental Colour to be paraded once a year. During the Korean War Royal Marines detachments at sea were also engaged in many bombardment actions and a number of Officers saw action as Fleet Air Arm pilots.

Chapter 7

More Brush Fire Wars
1952–1970

In May 1952 the Brigade returned to Malta from Malaya and in November the units received their first Colours from HRH The Duke of Edinburgh on Floriana Parade Ground, Valetta. Including Marines from the fleet and landing craft who kept the ground, there were sixty-seven Officers and 1,168 men on parade. In his address, Prince Philip, who was appointed Captain General the following year, said:

> *These Colours are a recognition of the devotion of the wartime Royal Marines Commandos and of the courage and bearing of the Brigade in all the trouble spots of the world since the war.'*

Although Royal Marines Commandos did not serve with the British Army of the Rhine, the Corps had a landing craft presence on the Rhine during the 1950s, when Royal Marines manned craft in the Rhine Squadron, but this was withdrawn from Germany in 1958.

It was not long before there was further unrest in the Suez Canal Zone and the whole Brigade, including the Headquarters, was sent there in May 1953 to carry out internal security duties, during which they were frequently sniped at by dissident Egyptians. The Brigade returned to Malta late in 1954, with 42 Commando continuing on to the UK to take over Commando Training at Bickleigh. In Cyprus EOKA terrorists, claiming a union with Greece, were now causing trouble. In September 1955, at forty-eight hours' notice, Brigade HQ, 40 and 45 Commandos were hastily embarked in HM Ships as part of a build-up of troops sent to the island to combat the serious disturbances. In August 1956 President Nasser of Egypt nationalised the Suez Canal. Once again the Brigade moved at short notice in HM Ships, this time to concentrate back in Malta. Meanwhile the operational nucleus of 42 Commando was quickly brought up to strength and went out to join the Brigade. With the Amphibious Warfare Squadron also based on Malta augmented by ships brought out of reserve, 3 Commando Brigade was ready for the amphibious

Port Said with the Suez Canal and showing the beaches where
40 and 42 Commandos landed on 6 November 1956.

assault on Port Said, Operation MUSKETEER.

On 6 November 40 and 42 Commandos, supported by 6 Royal Tank Regiment stormed the beaches of Port Said in LVTs and LCAs under cover of heavy naval bombardment with the Fleet Air Arm strafing Egyptian positions. Once their first objectives had been taken against light opposition, 45 Commando were landed by naval helicopters from the training carriers *Ocean* and *Theseus* in the first ever helicopter assault. Heavy street fighting continued and by late that day the Commandos had seized the port and joined up with 3 Battalion Parachute Regiment who had taken Gamil airfield the night before. What had been a highly successful military operation was brought to a sudden end by politicians in London calling a cease-fire at midnight. Ten Royal Marines had been killed in action. When troops were withdrawn and relieved by a United Nations force, 3 Commando Brigade returned to Malta and later 42 Commando, aboard HMS *Ocean* went back to UK where they arrived just before Christmas. The following year an enlarged Troop of over one hundred men from the unit spent eight months in Londonderry on anti-IRA patrols.

Cyprus

For the next two years 40 and 45 Commandos, based in Malta, were continually engaged on a rotation basis in anti-terrorist operations in Cyprus against rebel General Grivas' EOKA guerrillas, much of it in the inhospitable Troodos mountains. It was at this time that, following on from the success of its helicopter assault at Port Said 45 Commando formed 'Heliforce', consisting of two rifle troops and a flight of four Fleet Air Arm Whirlwind helicopters. The Port Said operation had demonstrated the flexibility of carrier borne helicopter operations. The United States had already developed helicopter techniques in Korea and the French had made use of the concept in North Africa.

45 Commando searching a village in the Troodos Mountains, Cyprus 1958.

Operation MUSKETEER had an uplifting effect on the future of the Corps and the amphibious assault concept of The Second World War came under scrutiny. The Defence White Paper of 1957 announced huge cuts in expenditure and manpower, the ending of National Service and a greater reliance on nuclear weapons for the defence of Europe. However it also saw the birth of the Commando Ship concept, particularly designed for operations outside Europe and, as far the Corps was concerned, mainly in the Far East.

HMS *Bulwark* was designated the first Commando Ship and commissioned with 848 Naval Air Squadron at the end of 1959 and on 14th March 1960, 42 Commando, brought up to strength, embarked for the Far East. The following year work began on converting HMS *Albion* as a second Commando ship; and in October that year 41 Commando was the first commando unit to reorganise from five 'fighting troops' to three rifle companies. One by one the other units followed suit over the next twelve months.

Royal Marines emplaning in helicopters aboard HMS *Bulwark*, the first Commando ship.

Aden

In 1960, 45 Commando moved to Aden in what was to be a tour lasting seven years of internal security operations in the Aden Protectorate and a bitter struggle during the long drawn out campaign in the mountains of the Radfan. There was a short operation in 1961 by both 45 Commando from Aden and 42 Commando from Singapore in support of Kuwait illustrating the remarkable flexibility and capability

71

45 Commando in the Radfan being resupplied by
Beaver and Twin Pioneer aircraft at Monks Field, 1963.

of this new amphibious concept. In 1964, when Army mutinies in the newly independent East African nations broke out, 45 Commando embarked in the light fleet carrier HMS *Centaur*, and stood by off the coast ready to aid Zanzibar and Tanganyika. The Commando was airlifted ashore when called for and surprised the dissident military with the swiftness of their helicopter operations. On their

Royal Marines in Oman from Persian Gulf frigates
in 1958 at the time of the Jebel Akdhar War to bolster the
Sultan's Armed Forces. They were the forerunners of hundreds
of Royal Marines to serve by sea, land and air in the SAF.

return to Aden for operations in the Radfan, '45' were relieved by 41 Commando, which had been flown out to Kenya from the UK. When the final withdrawal from Aden was announced in 1967, 42 Commando embarked in *Albion*, arrived from Singapore, and 45 Commando was flown back to UK. The two Commandos were the last units to leave the beleaguered former colony on 29th November.

Confrontation in Borneo

Also in 1961 Headquarters 3 Commando Brigade had left Malta for Singapore to be joined in 1962 by 40 Commando. It was not long before they were called on once again when the Brunei revolt erupted on 8 December 1962. 42 Commando were among the first to be flown across and L Company, under Captain Jeremy Moore, were immediately ordered to Limbang, 10 miles up river in Sarawak, where rebels had seized the British Resident, his wife and a dozen other hostages. Assisted by sailors from the minesweepers HMS *Fiskerton* and *Chawton*, they commandeered two Z craft and sailed up the river arriving off Limbang before dawn on 12 December. After being greeted by machine gun and rifle fire they ran into the beach and in a sharp engagement not only disposed of the rebels but also rescued all the hostages alive. Meanwhile Albion, which had been exercising with 40 Commando off the coast of East Africa raced across to deliver the unit into Sarawak by 14 December.

The Indonesian confrontation lasted nearly four years and for much of 1963 HQ 3 Commando Brigade, and its two commandos, supported initially by Royal Naval helicopter squadrons and later by the RAF, carried out rotating tours of duty in jungle fighting against insurgent Indonesian opposition. The Royal Marines Commandos, along with eight Gurkha battalions bore the brunt of the Borneo campaign and between December 1962 and September 1966 there was always at least one commando deployed there. Like all jungle operations,

A Commando stick landing from a Wessex helicopter in Borneo 1966.

contacts were rare but an extremely high state of alertness was essential at all times. The Corps lost sixteen killed and twenty wounded.

In 1964 the Corps celebrated its Tercentenary. Amongst a number of events held in July Her Majesty The Queen dined with the Officers in the Painted Hall of the Royal Naval College Greenwich. Earlier in the day she reviewed a representative parade in the grounds of Buckingham Palace. It was at this parade that one contingent wore Lovat uniform for the first time. She said:

> For 300 years the Royal Marines have served their country with devotion and courage. I am confident that, as long as Britain needs to be defended and to play a part in preserving peace throughout the world, they will have an honoured place in the armed forces of the Realm.

Other celebratory events were held wherever Royal Marines were serving. On the last day of Tercentery Year, 27 October 1965, Admiral of the Fleet, the Earl Mountbatten of Burma, who for many years had been a staunch supporter of the Corps, was honoured in a unique manner by being appointed the first Colonel Commandant for life.

The Tercentenary Review of the Royal Marines by HM The Queen at Buckingham Palace, 1964.

Two decades had passed since the end of the war and the Royal Marines had not only found new roles in Commandos, landing craft and in the Special Boat Squadron but had acquitted itself with professionalism around the Globe in the many 'brush fire wars'. The old RN landing craft base at Poole became a Royal Marines establishment in 1954, when the Amphibious School moved there and was joined by the Technical Training Wing in 1973, both from Fort Cumberland at Eastney. Also in 1973, as part of the run down and eventual closure of Eastney Barracks, the Signals Training Wing moved to Lympstone, which had become the Commando Training Centre in 1970 and also absorbed recruit training from the Depot at Deal in 1976.

HRH The Duke of Edinburgh, Captain General RM with his uncle, the Earl Mountbatten of Burma after the latter's installation as a Colonel Commandant RM

Chapter 8

The End of the Empire
1970–1981

By 1967 the end of the British Empire was dawning, former colonies and dependencies were being granted independence and there was no longer a need for a major British presence east of Suez. During the sixties both 41 and 43 Commandos had been reactivated for short spells, Portsmouth and Plymouth Groups had been reorganised as functional commands and the Corps strength stood at just over eight thousand, of whom eight hundred were in the Band Service. RM Detachments had been removed from the few remaining capital ships, but they were retained in certain vessels such as the ice patrol ship, HMS *Endurance*, and the Royal Yacht, *Britannia*. For a period, small twenty-two man detachments were embarked in frigates with a subaltern as OCRM and a Sergeant as the Sergeant Major, but even they were later reduced to only ten men under a SNCO, before being removed altogether by 1997.

Since leaving Aden in 1967, 45 Commando settled into Stonehouse Barracks, Plymouth and took up their new role in the Strategic Reserve. 3 Commando Brigade withdrew from the Far East in 1971 with a joint farewell parade in HMS

The Royal Yacht Band aboard SS *Gothic* during the Royal Tour 1953/54.

Simbang on 18 March, when at sunset the White Ensign was hauled down for the last time. 42 Commando was the first unit to return, settling into Bickleigh Barracks on 19th July. Headquarters 3 Commando Brigade followed taking up residence in Stonehouse Barracks, Plymouth, while 40 Commando, which had managed a short spell of duty in Hong Kong the previous year, arrived home just in time for Christmas 1971 and, returning from leave after the New Year, moved into Seaton Barracks, Plymouth. 45 Commando had moved up to Scotland in the spring of 1971 and took over the old RN Air Station at Arbroath. It was at this time that serious thought was given to establishing a Defence School of Music for all three services based on the Royal Marines School of Music at Deal. However, after a lengthy examination the idea was dropped but the future of Eastney Barracks was also under discussion and eventually an announcement made that the unit there would close. In 1973 the Drafting, Pay and Records Office, Royal Marines (DPRORM) was absorbed into HMS *Centurion* at Gosport, and by 1991 the Corps Museum at Eastney was left, for the time being, as the only Royal Marines presence in Portsmouth.

Just prior to leaving the Far East, elements of 3 Commando Brigade aboard HMS *Bulwark, Intrepid* and the LSL Sir *Galahad* had raced to a major flood disaster in East Pakistan (now Bangladesh) and carried out important relief work. Meanwhile in the UK, 41 Commando, as the 'Spearhead Battalion', had embarked on the Corps' first emergency tour of duty in Ulster in September 1969 shortly after the troubles blew up there, to be followed by 45 Commando in 1970, fresh from their move to Scotland. Based in the Crumlin Road area of Belfast, 45 Commando saw some of the worst of the violence, a grim portent of the many years to come (*see The Ulster Problem on page 81*).

Major Reorganisation

In England there had been other new developments and events. Both 29 Regiment Royal Artillery from 1961, and 59 Independent Squadron Royal Engineers from 1968 had provided field support for 3 Commando Brigade in the Far East and had by now been designated 'Commando' having become an integral part of the Brigade. For many years the Brigade had relied on the Army for their principal logistic support and in 1971 various logistic sub-units were brought together to form the Commando Logistic Regiment, which also included a Medical Squadron largely composed of RN personnel. The Regiment became a Royal Marines unit in 1974, and was initially commanded alternately by a Royal Marines Officer and an Army Officer (RAOC, RCT or REME). All ranks in these supporting elements had to earn their green beret before their postings were confirmed. In 1974, both 41 Commando, then based in Malta, and 40 Commando, as the 'Spearhead Battalion', were deployed to Cyprus following the Turkish invasion of the island. Royal Marines detachments served in many of the frigates involved in the dispute with Iceland over fishing grounds in the mid-70s (known as the Cod War).

It was also at this time that the affiliation between the Corps and the Royal Netherlands Marine Corps became even closer. The RNLMC provided a fourth Arctic and Mountain Warfare trained rifle company, Whisky Company, for 45 Commando and the United Kingdom/Netherlands Landing Force was established. Today there remain two RNLMC Officers serving on exchange.

To celebrate the Silver Jubilee of HM The Queen in 1977, 42 Commando provided the main unit for the parade for Her Majesty on Plymouth Hoe on 5 August with other units providing displays. It was also that year that 41 Commando was due for disbandment but, having Trooped the Colour before

In her Silver Jubilee year HM The Queen reviewed the Royal Marines on Plymouth Hoe.

Lord Mountbatten in Malta as their final parade, the Unit returned to the UK only to be immediately reformed at Deal. The following year they carried out a six-month tour of Northern Ireland and then represented the Royal Marines when they carried out London Duties for only the second time in the history of the Corps. In addition to providing guards on Buckingham Palace and St James's Palace they also mounted guard at the Tower of London. This was followed by a UN tour in Cyprus. The Unit was finally disbanded in 1981.

Since the withdrawal of Britain's forces from most overseas bases, government policy led to a new and demanding role for the Royal Marines within NATO. For the early part of the 1970s the Corps principal commitment was to NATO's Southern Flank, the Mediterranean area, but also in 1970 the first Royal Marines unit, 45 Commando, acquired a mountain and arctic warfare role in Norway to support the Alliance's Northern Flank. By 1979 the whole of 3 Commando Brigade was committed to arctic warfare. In addition, Commandos took their turn with Army units for four-month, and occasionally twelve-month, tours in Northern Ireland (*see The Ulster Problem*), and also in Belize; they carried out United Nations tours in Cyprus in 1979 and 1984, and the tactical headquarters and one company of 42 Commando was sent at short notice to the New Hebrides (now Vanuatu) in 1980 to enforce independence, where it was contested. The Corps was now tasked with maritime security within the UK and its exclusive economic zone, becoming the established experts at the protection of offshore oil and gas installations, whilst units, both large and small, were always available for other operations outside the NATO area when required. The changing role of the Royal Navy saw a decrease in the size of detachments at sea and the advent of the integral ship's helicopter in the late 1960s had given sea-going Marines a new challenge.

In the realms of amphibious warfare, the Royal Navy and Royal Marines, together with the Royal Navy, had experienced the scrapping of the two LPHs (Landing Platform Helicopter) and the decision to scrap the two LPDs (Landing Platform Dock). By 1980 the strength of the Royal Marines was down to about 7,500 with the Royal Marines Reserve providing support with a further 1,000 men. The units of 3 Commando Brigade were stationed mainly in Devon, while 45 Commando was at Arbroath. The independent 41 Commando occupied Deal until it was disbanded in the following year. It was in May 1980 that Comacchio

Company (named after the The Second World War battle in Italy fought by 43 Commando) was formed at Arbroath. This Company, later expanded to become Comacchio Group and then renamed the Fleet Protection Group, assumed responsibility for the security of the nuclear deterrent and its associated facilities at HMNB Clyde. It also continued to develop the 'Oilsafe' techniques pioneered by L Company of 42 Commando in 1977 to safeguard Britain's offshore gas and oil installations. The Royal Marines also provided the Special Boat Squadron, based at Poole in Dorset, which since the war had been the experts in beach reconnaissance, underwater swimming, and had a wealth of experience in anti-terrorist operations.

Continuing Operations

In the autumn of 1979, 42 Commando completed an emergency tour in Hong Kong to help the British Forces stationed there in their role of assisting the Royal Hong Kong Police (RHKP) deal with an unprecedented illegal immigration crisis.

During their time in the colony, they pioneered the use of raiding craft in sea borne Anti-Illegal Immigrant (II) patrols. Their success in apprehending large numbers of IIs attempting the sea crossing persuaded the Hong Kong Government to ask for a continuing RM presence, and thus it was that in April 1980, 3 Raiding Squadron (3 RSRM) was born. Initially equipped with Avon Searider Rigid Inflatable Boats (RIBs), the Squadron found itself being increasingly outrun by faster speedboats.

The introduction from September 1984 of the Fast Pursuit Craft (FPC) allowed the Squadron to regain superior capability and in the first 6 months after its introduction, twenty-one 'Snakehead' speedboats were successfully intercepted. The Squadron comprised two Officers, a WO2, two SNCOs, thirty-one Corporals/Marines and twelve RN locally enlisted able seamen. Following declining levels of II activity and the increased capability of the RHKP Small Boat Unit, 3 RSRM was disbanded on 1st July 1988. They also assisted with several rescues and other incidents, including two when they came under fire. After disbandment, a small RM presence remained in Hong Kong with a Lieutenant and a Colour Sergeant joining the Staff of the Senior Officer Hong Kong Squadron to co-ordinate three 3-man detachments operating FPCs from

Ranks from 42 Commando searching a
Hong Kong fishing vessel for illegal immigrants, 1979

HM Ships *Peacock*, *Plover* and *Starling*. They remained there until the Colony was handed over to the Chinese in 1997, thus continuing a tradition of RM involvement in the territory that dated back to the possession of Hong Kong Island in 1841.

The Ulster Problem

Twentieth Century unrest in Ireland dates from its early decades when Royal Marines were twice sent to the south of the country; in 1916 to help quell the rebellion and again in 1922 when the 8th Battalion spent two years there. In 1957 elements of 42 Commando had spent eight months in Ulster on anti-IRA border patrols. It was in late September 1969 that 41 Commando, as 'Spearhead Battalion' and ready to move anywhere in the world at immediate notice, was sent to the Divis Street area of Belfast. The following year, 1970, saw 45 Commando arriving in Belfast on 1 June for the first of many tours in the province.

After that Royal Marines Commandos regularly took their turn with Army battalions and units in internal security operations in Ulster. From 1 March 1979, 40 Commando spent a year in Londonderry, based at Ballykelly, and was not very far away from where Admiral of the Fleet the Earl Mountbatten of Burma (and a Colonel Commandant of the Royal Marines) was brutally assassinated by the IRA, whilst holidaying with his family at Mullaghmore on 27 August.

In the early days there was little or no special internal security equipment and the military had to face their tormentors unprotected even by batons and shields. The Marines lived in rough quarters, their sleeping bags being crowded into large rooms, or even garden sheds. Sometimes these were factories, other times requisitioned schools. The Quartermaster and his staff, responsible for the supply of rations, clothing and ammunition, had only unarmoured vehicles in which to visit the outlying company locations. Protective clothing was slowly developed through the 1970s when flak jackets and special helmets with visors were introduced. Gloves and other specialist clothing, new weapons, anti-riot shields and CS grenades were brought into use. Later still night vision equipment was developed, giving better surveillance capability at night. Armoured personnel carriers were used for transit whilst Landrovers and other light vehicles were protected with armour and wire mesh. The terrorists became more sophisticated in their methods and counter measures were devised against such weapons as improvised mortars and electrically initiated mines that restricted movement, other than on foot, to helicopters in high risk areas. Patrolling was initially done on foot in four-man groups. As there was no need for heavier weapons, the Marines of Support Company and Gunners from associated Royal Artillery batteries became foot soldiers. Each Commando would develop its own tactics and drills for dealing with its own particular area. On occasions Commandos were based in the built-up areas of Belfast and Londonderry, at other times on the border in South Armagh, where completely different tactics were evolved.

Wearing flak jackets, the Band of Commando Forces entertains in Belfast City Centre, 1972.

On 31st July 1972, 22,000 British troops were involved in Ulster in Operation MOTORMAN that

Marine of 42 Commando makes friends with a young Irish lad
during a patrol in Crossmaglen, 1984.

successfully cleared the 'no-go' areas of West Belfast and Londonderry. Royal Marines and Royal Naval personnel manned the four landing craft that took Royal Engineers bulldozers up the River Foyle into the heart of Londonderry. 40, 42 and 45 Commandos were involved. The saturation of the Catholic districts of both cities forced the terrorists to relinquish control, and allowed the security forces to move into a new phase of the campaign. Knowing they were up against a professional enemy, every man had to remain fully alert at all times, prepared for the unexpected, the sniper, the carefully laid bomb or the ambush.

The troubles did not only affect the Corps deployed to Northern Ireland for in 1981 an attempt was made on the life of the Commandant General Royal Marines, Lieutenant General Sir Steuart Pringle, whose car was blown up by a terrorist bomb outside his London home and he suffered serious injuries. Much later, on 22nd September 1989, eleven Royal Marines musicians were murdered when a bomb was planted at the Royal Marines School of Music at Deal.

During this time, emphasis had been given to long-term intelligence and patrolling, winning the hearts and minds of these complex people, divided by their own religious beliefs. Patrolling the streets or countryside was a lonely and difficult task when the civilian population was trying to live as normal a life as possible. It was a frustrating and bitter struggle that the security forces were engaged in. It was often difficult for the Marine who came from the mainland to understand the inbred hostility that existed between the various factions in Ulster. But this was just another job for which the regular serviceman had to be trained, learning new skills to meet the special demands of fighting terrorism.

Royal Marines Commandos carried out more than 40 tours (the last in 2004) and they lost sixteen killed (plus the musicians at Deal) and ninety-five wounded in those bleak years. Until a political solution was found in 2007, there was no real peace in the Province. The late 1970s had seen successive cutbacks in British defence forces, but in 1981 the Government Defence White Paper threatened to reduce the Royal Navy to little more than an anti-submarine force for the North Atlantic, and the Corps was once again threatened. When the Argentines invaded the Falkland Islands in the following year, it presented the Corps with an amphibious task for which they were highly suited.

This memorial, to the eleven band ranks killed when an IRA bomb exploded at the RM School of Music in 1989, now stands in a Garden of Rest adjacent to the site of the old Concert Hall in Canada Road at Deal, which was burnt down in 2003.

Chapter 9

The Falklands War

1982

3 Commando Brigade was immediately despatched to the South Atlantic and played a major part in the recapture of the Falklands. Over fifty percent of the total Royal Marines strength of 7,500 men were involved in the Falklands War. It was the perfect scenario for the sea-soldier, now turned commando, with an amphibious assault, a rugged approach march and a tough final battle in adverse conditions of both weather and terrain. Royal Marines were engaged in all phases of the campaign. They served as detachments in many HM Ships, as crews of landing craft, as commandos on the ground and as light helicopter pilots in the air. The Special Boat Squadron carried out highly important surveillance and reconnaissance. It was total involvement by the Corps.

The Royal Marines had provided a small garrison in the Falkland Islands at various times in the 19th Century. HM Ships landed their detachments there regularly in the 1940s and 50s, but in 1965 Naval Party 8901 (NP 8901)

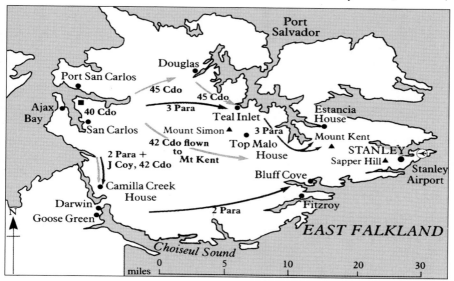

was established. This was a permanent Royal Marines garrison and in 1982 numbered thirty-seven all ranks. Men normally did a one-year tour but many volunteered for a second tour in this small dependency two hundred miles off the Argentine coast. Others married local girls on leaving the Service and settled there. Such was the Royal Marines background to the invasion of the islands by the Argentines on the night of 1/2 April 1982.

It was mere coincidence that the force was double its normal size as the new NP 8901 had just arrived to take over from their predecessors. When first indications of an Argentine invasion were received, the Royal Marines prepared their defences, particularly in the airport area and around government buildings. With an area equivalent to that of Wales and a coastline three times as long, it was impossible to defend, or even observe, more than small stretches.

Argentine Special Forces landed in the early hours of 2 April, taking a cross-country route to make a devastating attack on the Marines base, which had been evacuated a few hours earlier. Soon after first light one thousand assault troops with armoured personnel carriers swamped the town. There was some brief resistance from the Marines but, in view of the overwhelming odds, Governor Rex Hunt ordered the Royal Marines to surrender to avoid civilian casualties. Earlier in March HMS Endurance had landed her RM detachment to watch a party of Argentine scrap metal merchants on South Georgia, eight hundred miles east of the Falklands. The detachment based itself alongside the British Antarctic Survey Base at Grytviken. On 3 April the Argentines also attacked the island and after two and a half hours fighting, in which an enemy helicopter was shot down and a corvette hit, the Marines were forced to give in against overwhelming opposition.

Within twenty-four hours of the Argentine invasion, the first British warships sailed south as a preliminary to the re-occupation of the islands. An Amphibious Task Group sailed within a week carrying the whole of 3 Commando Brigade, including its own Gunners and Sappers, plus 2nd and 3rd Battalions of the Parachute Regiment, combining to form the toughest fighting force in the world. Although many men had been on Easter leave and some were holidaying abroad, the whole force was ready to embark within seventy-two hours. In addition to the fighting element, the Commando Logistic Regiment and RN Surgical Support Teams supported the initial infantry force, along with the Commando Forces

RM Band who provided stretcher-bearers and personnel for other tasks afloat and were also a morale boosting bonus. Two Troops of the Blues and Royals with Scorpion and Scimitar light tanks, and T Battery of 12 Air Defence Regiment RA with their Rapier missiles, a battery of 4 Field Regiment RA and a troop of 9 Parachute Squadron RE made up the remainder of the landing force.

Over 3,500 miles from Britain and halfway to the Falklands, the main Amphibious Task Group stopped off at Ascension Island to train, shake down and cross-load. 40 and 42 Commandos, with 3 Para, were embarked in the SS Canberra, one of forty-nine civilian ships taken up from trade (STUFT). This equalled the number of HM Ships eventually involved in the campaign. Other units were in amphibious ships and Royal Fleet Auxiliaries. Amongst the stores were about seventy-five over-snow vehicles but little other transport was taken.

M Company Group of 42 Commando, with SAS and SBS backing, had recaptured South Georgia by 25 April supported by HMS *Antrim* and *Plymouth*. After initial reconnaissance by Special Forces in appalling weather, the main attacking force was landed a short distance from Grytviken, and under the cover of a naval bombardment, advanced upon the Argentines and forced them to surrender.

The Landing Force was commanded by the Commander 3 Commando

M Company 42 Commando searching Grytviken,
South Georgia during the Falklands Campaign, 1982.

Brigade, Brigadier Julian Thompson who, with Commodore Mike Clapp (Amphibious Task Group Commander) became responsible for the detailed planning of the assault. The Task Force Commander was Admiral Sir John Fieldhouse, working from his headquarters in Northwood, Middlesex, while Rear Admiral 'Sandy' Woodward commanded the Carrier Battle Task Group, operating in the South Atlantic. Later, when 5 Infantry Brigade were sent south, Major General Jeremy Moore, the Royal Marines most decorated serving Officer, became the Land Forces Commander, Falklands Islands. Detailed planning of the options for landing took place whilst the Task Force was at Ascension Island. However members of the Special Boat Squadron and the Army's Special Air Service had been landed secretly from submarines and helicopters from small ships from 1 May. Their task was to glean intelligence and information about the Argentine Forces, their strength and dispositions, and report. Many spent more than three weeks living in the open in appalling weather, in close proximity to the enemy. The special SBS task was to reconnoitre beaches, reporting on gradients, hinterland, and suitability for landing an enlarged Brigade.

Operations at sea, which included the sinking of the Argentine cruiser *General Belgrano*, and the loss of the destroyer HMS *Sheffield*, continued in the cold waters of the South Atlantic. In the air, Fleet Air Arm Sea Harriers patrolled the skies above the Fleet while remarkable long range bombing raids were carried out on Stanley airfield by Vulcan bombers from the UK, involving six in-flight refuellings.

At dawn on 21 May, 3 Commando Brigade carried out a virtually unopposed landing in the San Carlos Settlement on the west coast of East Falkland. It took six days to whittle down the Argentine Air Force but the determined enemy from the mainland two hundred miles away continued to cause considerable concern and damage to the ships and ground forces. 45 Commando landed at Ajax Bay, 40 Commando and 2 Para at San Carlos Settlement, and 3 Para at Port San Carlos. 42 Commando initially remained afloat as the Brigade reserve, landing later that day. During the landings two RM Gazelle helicopters were shot down with the loss of three crewmen.

After consolidating for five days, including setting up a Brigade Maintenance Area and Field Dressing Station at Ajax Bay, 3 Commando Brigade began to break out from the bridgehead on 26/27 May. 2 Para moved south to attack

Goose Green on 28 May. This was a bloody battle against considerable odds during which the Commanding Officer, Lieutenant Colonel 'H' Jones, was killed and later awarded a posthumous Victoria Cross.

Whilst this action was taking place, 45 Commando, 550 men, started their long 'yomp' across East Falkland, through Douglas settlement to Teal Inlet. Their thirty-five mile route lay across some of the most forbidding country in the world. Ankle deep bogs, valleys of knee twisting grass and rock runs of boulders were covered in fourteen hours with few stops and without sleep. Men carried up to fifty kilogrammes on their backs, their own equipment weighted down with spare mortar ammunition. Meanwhile 3 Para took a more southerly cross-country course to Teal Inlet. 40 Commando, much to their disappointment, were left to provide the defence for San Carlos.

Between 30 May and 5 June, 45 Commando and 3 Para moved forward to positions in the area of Mount Kent and Mount Estancia. Meanwhile 42 Commando had been flown forward by helicopters on the nights of 30/31 May and 31 May/1 June to take up positions on Mount Kent. From here the Commando moved to Mount Challenger. From these positions all units carried out a vigorous patrolling programme to dominate 'no man's land', and fix the Argentine positions.

On 30 May, 5 Infantry Brigade (2 Scots Guards, 1 Welsh Guards and 1/7

45 Commando pass through Port San Carlos prior to their 'yomp' across East Falkland.

Gurkha Rifles) had arrived off San Carlos and Major General Jeremy Moore, the Land Forces Commander, came ashore to the beachhead. It was during 5 Infantry Brigade's subsequent move forward by sea to advanced positions at Fitzroy that enemy aircraft attacked the LSL RFA Sir Galahad in Bluff Cove causing casualties of fifty killed and sixty wounded, many of them from the Welsh Guards.

There was a sharp engagement near Top Malo House when nineteen members of the Mountain & Arctic Warfare Cadre, operating in a reconnaissance role, attacked Argentine Forces, killing five and taking the remaining twelve captive, seven of whom were wounded, an excellent example of good planning, intelligence and execution.

For the next ten days, continuous patrolling by the forward units built up a detailed intelligence picture of the enemy defences and dispositions. Royal Engineers and Royal Marines assault engineers recced and mapped enemy minefields, while gunners of 29 Commando Regiment and 4 Field Regiment pounded enemy defences around Stanley controlled by their own and Naval Gunfire Forward Observers. RAF and Fleet Air Arm helicopters brought up stocks of stores and ammunition. The enemy, consisting of the well trained 5th Marine Regiment and the conscripted 4th, 6th and 7th Infantry Regiments, held strong positions on the barren, craggy hilltops. They were badly led in most cases, but still proved tough opposition.

Plans for a final co-ordinated Brigade night attack were laid and tasks were given as follows: 3 Para – Mount Longdon (to the north); 45 Commando – Two Sisters (centre); 42 Commando – Mount Harriet (in the south); all units would exploit forward if possible. 2 Para and units of 5 Infantry Brigade were held in reserve. The assault was launched on the night of 11/12 June; initially it was a silent approach, but later as the attackers neared their targets they brought down a barrage of naval gunfire, artillery and mortars.

The assaults were made uphill over open ground covered with strafing machine gun fire. 42 Commando did a daring encircling movement to catch the enemy on Mount Harriet in the rear; 3 Para had a tougher time before taking Mount Longdon against the Argentine Marines when Sergeant Ian McKay was awarded a posthumous Victoria Cross; and 45 Commando had the difficult task of a flanking attack and then thrusting along a narrow ridge to the twin peaks of Two Sisters. By dawn, all the objectives had been taken, but the troops were exhausted and exploitation forward had to be left to fresh units.

The Argentine defenders were beginning to lose the will to fight. However there was one hurdle left before the lights of Stanley could be seen. On the night of 13/14 June, 2 Para took Wireless Ridge to the north supported by two light tanks of the Blues and Royals without much trouble, but the Scots Guards faced the tougher task of capturing Tumbledown Mountain in a bloody eleven-hour battle.

By dawn, defeated Argentines were seen wending their way back into Stanley and white flags were prominent. At 1105 on 14 June the British troops were ordered to fire only in self-defence and the weary, battle-worn 'veterans' marched into Stanley. General Moore finally took the Argentine unconditional surrender in Stanley at 0900 hours that evening. Nearly thirteen thousand prisoners were taken and repatriated to Argentina within the next few days, whilst the British Marines and Paras sailed slowly home in the luxury and comfort of modern ships. When SS Canberra sailed into Southampton Water on a sunny Sunday morning of 11 July it was to a euphoric homecoming. The sheer scale of the welcome took them by surprise.

The Falklands War was but a short campaign. To mount a force to re-occupy

40 Commando round up Argentine prisoners of war at Port Howard in West Falkland.

a group of islands seven thousand miles away in the South Atlantic, within range of the enemy air force, was a remarkable achievement, which showed versatility, determination, flexibility and a high degree of military professionalism. The calculated decision to send a British Task Force to protect sovereign rights and the freedom of the individual against unprovoked aggression was undoubtedly fully justified. The cost was 255 British lives and 750 Argentines lost. The Royal Marines had lost twenty-six killed and added another feat of arms to its already illustrious amphibious history.

As a result of the Falklands war the government eventually drastically changed its naval policy, particularly regarding its surface fleet, and the Royal Marines grew in strength from this, although there was no increase in numbers.

Another Change of Direction

In August 1982, the first Royal Marines detachment was sent to Diego Garcia in the Indian Ocean for security duties, and where they doubled up their military role with appointments as civil police and customs Officers. There were also commando exercises in Norway and Brunei. 40 Commando which had moved into its new home in Taunton in 1983, spent four months as part of the UN peace-keeping force in Cyprus the following spring, and in September 1985 started an eight month tour in Belize.

It was in 1986 that the new SA80 rifle was introduced into the Corps and 42 Commando had the honour of being the first unit to carry out Public Duties in London armed with this weapon, mounting guards on Buckingham Palace, St James's Palace, the Tower of London and on this occasion Windsor Castle also.

On the operational front Royal Marines served in frigates of the Armilla Patrol in the Persian Gulf. This was the codename for the operation to escort and protect British ships in and out of the Persian Gulf, and between 1986 and 1988 some 1,020 ships were given this safeguard. On 23 January 1986 HM Royal Yacht *Britannia*, with the RM Band and a small detachment embarked, was involved in the dramatic evacuation of over one thousand British nationals from Aden during heavy fighting between Marxist elements in the former British colony, now the People's Democratic Republic of Yemen.

The unification of Europe and the breaking down of the iron curtain in 1990 radically changed Britain's defence policy yet again. No longer were large military forces required to face the Warsaw Pact countries, and an emphasis was put on smaller, highly mobile military units ready to face any commitment at a moment's notice. This was just the sort of role that the Royal Marines cherish, with their highly skilled training where the emphasis is on physical fitness, individual initiative, mobility and adaptability.

The New Guard entering Buckingham Palace forecourt during
42 Commando's tour of duty in London, 1986.

Chapter 10
The Gulf War and a New Century
1983–2002

When Saddam Hussein ordered his Iraqi troops to invade Kuwait in August 1990, the British government was among the first to respond. Unlike the Falklands, this was an operation in which the Army and Royal Air Force would have the prime roles, with the Royal Navy being tasked to patrol the Persian Gulf. Although the United States provided the majority of the forces, the United Kingdom played the second most important role in the multi-national United Nations force.

At first the British response was limited to Naval and Air Forces to deter

A boarding party exercise.

the Iraqi Forces moving on from Kuwait to Saudi Arabia or other Gulf countries. Royal Marines Air Defence detachments joined the Royal Navy's Armilla Patrol ships within hours of being ordered to move; these were followed quickly by Protection Teams for the naval boarding parties as the United Nations authorised economic sanctions. All these teams, using rigid inflatable boats to enable boarding to take place while target vessels remained underway, and Lynx helicopters to rope down onto ships, spearheaded the embargo efforts, preventing Iraq from receiving proscribed goods from the outside world.

As the United Kingdom contribution to the coalition grew so the Royal Marines involvement increased with substantial presence in the Allied Headquarters; security teams for the Royal Fleet Auxiliary vessels; the Royal Marines Band of the Commander-in-Chief Fleet on board the Primary Casualty Receiving Ship, RFA Argus, as stretcher bearers and medical orderlies; landing craft to assist in Mine Counter Measures operations; medical teams in the land based Field Hospitals; and men in the Naval Commando Helicopter Squadrons based in Saudi Arabia. In all, ten percent of the Corps was involved in Operation GRANBY.

When the fighting war had finished, the focus of attention turned to the plight of the Kurdish refugees who were fleeing from the retribution being handed out by the Iraqi Army. British Forces soon became involved in providing humanitarian assistance and protection to the hundreds of thousands of Kurds who had fled to the mountains along the Turkish/Iraqi border. Operation HAVEN, spearheaded by 3 Commando Brigade Royal Marines had begun.

In a situation reminiscent of the Falklands crisis, the Brigade Commander was in Norway when 3 Commando Brigade was earmarked (in 1982 he had been in Denmark). He returned, was briefed and flew to Turkey with his recce group to be followed quickly by the advance parties from 45 Commando, 40 Commando, the Commando Logistic Regiment and from the 1st Amphibious Combat Group (1 ACG) of the Royal Netherlands Marine Corps. The latter were a welcome addition to the Brigade, cementing relationships that stretched back over twenty years and which were unique in NATO. Within days 45 Commando were spearheading the move into Iraq to create the safe havens for Kurdish refugees. The speed of the operation was no more vividly demonstrated than by the men of 45 Commando who were on post-Northern Ireland leave one week, in Turkey the next and moving into Iraq the following! In all over four thousand British troops from all three services were involved with the 2,500 Royal Marines providing the fighting element. Major General Robert Ross, (MGRM Commando Forces) was nominated as Joint Force Commander in Turkey with the Force made up of Naval Sea King helicopters, 3 Commando Brigade (with its normal helicopters, artillery, engineer and logistic support), 1

A Royal Marine is subjected to close scrutiny by a Zakhu resident in Northern Iraq during
Operation HAVEN, 1991.

ACG and a battalion of Dutch engineers, and a medical team from Australia
plus Hercules transports and Chinook helicopters from the RAF.

With disease spreading fast amongst the refugees in the wintry conditions
of northern Iraq, the provision of shelter, food, water and medical supplies were
the first considerations. The next concern was to encourage the Kurdish refugees
to return either to United Nations controlled camps or their own homes. A firm
liaison was built up between the forces and the British Overseas Development
Agency volunteers.

Royal Marines turned their hands to these unusual tasks with enthusiasm
and compassion, an essential quality in any serviceman. With 40 Commando
providing emergency relief in the mountain refugee camps and 45 Commando
and 1 ACG providing security in the safe havens, gradually the Kurds were
coaxed down from their mountain camps and persuaded that it was safe to return
to their homes.

By 15 July 1991, all the forces had withdrawn and a brittle peace had
been restored. The three months had been very hard but satisfying work. 40

Commando left a company behind as part of the multi-national 'Rainbow Battalion', deployed in Eastern Turkey as a deterrent to any Iraqi aggression towards the Kurdish people. They finally withdrew in September 1991.

These operations highlighted the remarkable skills of the Royal Marines in changing quickly from an aggressive fighting force to a compassionate peace keeping force. It showed yet again how swiftly the Corps can react in a time of crisis and how important are initiative, diplomacy and versatility. These are all part of the make-up of the modern Royal Marine.

Towards the Twenty-First Century

1998 was the year of the Strategic Defence Review that was particularly significant for the Corps: while many arms of the Services saw yet more cuts, a clear commitment was given to maintaining a national brigade-sized landing force, with the necessary associated shipping. By the turn of the century this endorsement had borne fruit in the shape of a variety of new ships and systems, either planned or imminent. In this year too the Corps was involved in an operation which in retrospect seems to have demonstrated the type of deployment of the future.

40 Commando embarked in HMS Ocean in Plymouth Sound.

97

40 Commando took part in Operation LADBROOK in the Congo Republic. Arriving in Brazzaville via Ascension Island, they were prepared to assist in the evacuation of British nationals from Kinshasa in the Democratic Republic of Congo. In the event, they were not used, but it demonstrated once again the Corps ability to move men quickly, with assets such as hovercraft, to wherever they were wanted. Before two years were out the Corps was to return again to this troubled continent.

The break-up of the Former Republic of Yugoslavia was a key feature of European politics in the 1990s, and the Corps still continued to be involved there in the new Century. In 1995 Major General David Pennefather was appointed Commander Rapid Reaction Force Operations Staff in Bosnia Herzegovina with seventy-four Officers and men. Royal Marines were involved throughout this conflict, as Liaison Officers, as United Nations observers, and in Public Relations duties.

The Millennial Year underlined the part the Corps plays in the defence arena, with some seventy-eight percent of the Corps on operations at one point, and with exercises or deployments in thirty different countries. The many and varied tasks carried out in this year typify the challenges which resulted from the changing world order in the 1990s. They are of a nature in many ways very different from previous years, and give a pointer to the future.

The Commando Brigade maintained its role as a very high readiness formation available as part of the national Joint Rapid Reaction Force, which was set up in 1999. The Headquarters itself, supported by its Signal Squadron, and a Royal Marines Band, deployed to Kosovo in command of the Multi-National Brigade (Centre), with the task of supporting the UN Mission in Kosovo in attempting to restore order following the withdrawal of the Yugoslav Army; violence was endemic with Albanians settling scores with Serbs, and with turf wars developing between rival Albanian gangs.

The Headquarters commanded some eighteen units, including 45 Commando, the Commando Logistic Regiment, a British infantry battalion, Royal Artillery and Royal Engineer units, and Swedish, Finnish and Norwegian battalions. 45 Commando had just returned home from six weeks jungle training in Belize before deploying to Kosovo, where they took over a base in the town of Pristina. Here progress was made in developing a police force and a credible judicial system, all against a background of intimidation and abduction of officials, armed robbery, and vandalism. The backdrop of political uncertainty surrounding the demise of the infamous President Milosevic provided an interesting run-up to the Kosovo elections, which were held in a benign environment, in no small way due to the efforts of 45 Commando and the rest of the multi-national brigade.

42 Commando provided the Corps main contribution to the Joint Rapid Reaction Force from April 2000 onwards. In March an Amphibious Ready Group (ARG) consisting of HMS *Ocean*, *Fearless* and support shipping sailed to the Mediterranean with the Commando Group embarked. After training in Portugal and France with NATO allies, plans changed in May due to events in Sierra Leone.

Here, there was a serious threat to the Government by the Revolutionary United Front, one of many rebel movements that was supported by neighbouring countries which coveted Sierra Leone's rich mineral resources, in particular, the diamond fields. Some four hundred UN Observers, including some Royal Marines, were surrounded and taken hostage.

The ARG was diverted to play a leading part in the Joint UK Force deployed to help stabilise the situation and support the UN Force there: the largest

A patrol of 40 Commando in Sierra Leone, 2000.

Naval Task Force since the Falklands War assembled offshore for Operation PALLISER. Only seven days had elapsed between re-embarkation of the ARG in France, sailing via Gibraltar and Dakar (where stores and men were embarked, and training undertaken) and arrival on task in Sierra Leone, when after being poised offshore they relieved First Battalion, The Parachute Regiment. Intensive patrolling took place both on land, to keep the rebels away from the airhead at Lungi, and on the rivers using Ocean's landing craft from 9 Assault Squadron and hovercraft from 539 Assault Squadron. In addition training support was provided to the Sierra Leone Army. Having returned to UK, the Commando Group joined the ARG again to conduct exercises in Gibraltar, Ukraine and Turkey. In October the call to arms came again, and they found themselves en route to Sierra Leone for the second time in six months. An eight day operation (Operation SILKMAN) gave them time to demonstrate the considerable firepower available to the Commando, and so issue a timely warning to the dissident forces opposing the UN.

Commando Structural Changes

Since the end of the Cold War in 1989, changes in the global security situation and Government policy had meant that the operational situations in which the Corps might find itself had dramatically changed. With a range of new equipment coming into service that would increase the firepower and mobility of Royal Marines units, such as that provided by the .5 inch heavy machine gun and the 'Viking All-Terrain Vehicle', and with the advent of a new generation of amphibious shipping, there was a need to optimise the Brigade's ability to meet its tasks. A study was undertaken which resulted in a major reorganisation of the Commando unit structure. It had not markedly altered since the change to rifle companies from the original troop organisation in the early 1960s. 'Commando 21' was conceived as a result of lessons learnt from previous operations and recent operational analysis; Commando units were restructured in the period 2000–2003 to allow them to hit harder, faster and more accurately.

In 2000, having just spent six months supporting the Royal Ulster Constabulary in Belfast from their home base in Taunton, 40 Commando reorganised into this new 'Commando 21' structure, followed in successive years by the other two Commandos. This organisation was needed to take advantage of modern weapon systems, enhanced firepower and greater mobility, and to cope with the increasing pace of contemporary operations.

Closer Links with the Royal Navy

Since 1998 there had no longer been RM detachments in ships in the Fleet. CINCFLEET suggested that the Royal Marines should provide a Fleet Standby Rifle Troop (FSRT) consisting of six six-man teams with a four-man HQ ready to support Fleet operations worldwide. These teams, which were originally provided by the Commando Units in turn, rapidly proved their worth and were constantly in demand. Amongst their many deployments they were aboard HMS *Cumberland* off Albania for possible evacuation of British nationals, in HMS *Cornwall* off Sierra Leone to protect British interests, and with HMS *Glasgow* off East Timor, where unrest followed the independence ballot in the capital Dili. In 2000 the task was added to those undertaken by Comacchio Group, whose main role remained the security of the national nuclear deterrent, but by now included amongst its other tasks was the provision of water-borne detachments in Northern Ireland, where they played a key part in securing the inland waterways and coastal areas. It had also become charged with the protection of the Fleet Headquarters at Northwood. In recognition of its changing and increased responsibilities the unit was re-titled the Fleet Protection Group in 2001 and moved from Condor Barracks, Arbroath, which it had shared with 45 Commando Group, to purpose built accommodation at Faslane.

This change of title of Comacchio Group epitomised the closer relationship of the Corps with the Royal Navy, and indeed the changing role of the Navy, as underlined by the concept of Littoral Warfare, and the increasing inventory of specialist amphibious ships. More staff appointments in the Corps became open to Naval Officers, and vice versa, with, for example, a Royal Marines Officer as Commander of a Naval shore establishment, and a Royal Navy Officer as Director of Training at Lympstone. In 1999 the decision was made to realign Royal Marines Officers' ranks with those of Officers of the Royal Navy and other services to remove existing ambiguity in corresponding rank. All serving Officers between Lieutenants of 3 years seniority and Lieutenant Colonels were moved one rank higher, thus ending years of confusion over exactly what ranks Royal Marines equated to in other services – confusion which most Officers had happily enjoyed. Perhaps the culmination of our integration with the Navy came in 2002 when HQRM in Portsmouth, the successor to the Department of the Commandant General in London, was integrated into the new Fleet Headquarters on Whale Island in Portsmouth.

Major Alterations to Corps Organisation

With the strength of the Corps gradually becoming smaller the rank of the Commandant General had also reduced. When General Sir Peter Whiteley was appointed C-in-C Allied Forces NW Europe in 1977, his relief as CGRM was a Lieutenant General, Sir John Richards. Similarly, when Lieutenant General Sir Robert Ross retired in 1996, his relief was a Major General. The appointment of Commandant General Royal Marines was eventually changed on 2nd April 2002, when it became secondary to his prime operational role as the Commander of United Kingdom Amphibious Forces (COMUKAMPHIBFOR), and as such was ready to deploy on operations and exercises with his battle staff. At the same time Headquarters Royal Marines, which had only existed as such for nine years, closed and was subsumed into the Fleet Headquarters; responsibility for Regimental affairs, individual training and the Reserves was vested in his deputed representative at Fleet Headquarters, a Colonel, with the appointment title of Director Royal Marines. This reorganisation gave the Corps the exciting opportunity to play a major role in the Joint Rapid Reaction Force. At this time too, the re-naming of Royal Marines Poole as 1 Assault Group RM more properly reflected its responsibility for training, parenting and co-ordinating all landing craft assets. RM Poole remains the name of the base at Poole.

The Royal Marines Band Service also moved with the times. Once more reduced numbers and less bands, coupled with an even higher standard of musical recruitment, has ensured they lead the world in the realms of military music, besides having an operational support role. In 2007, thirty percent of the Band Service of 350 (including seventy under training) were women, whose recruitment started in 1992. As musicians and buglers, and on operations, they play their part admirably, but recruitment of women into the General Service of the Corps is still unlikely in the near future.

Given the type of people the Corps attracts, and the ethos and attitude it imbues in its members, it comes as no surprise that many take the opportunity to test their courage and endurance in adventurous activities. Throughout the twentieth century, Royal Marines took part in such outdoor pursuits as regularly winning the Devizes to Westminster Canoe Race, the Three Peaks Race, mountaineering in the Himalayas, the ascent of K2, Mount McKinley in Alaska and single handed transatlantic sailing. In 2000 a Corporal and a Marine completed the first ever unsupported journey, on foot, to the North Pole, overcoming frostbite, exhaustion and appalling weather in the process. In 2001 two Corporals attempted to row across the Pacific, but at the five thousand mile point they were run down by a fishing boat – leading to strong words, apparently, with its skipper! 2003 saw a Royal Marine on the summit of Everest as a member of a joint RN/RM expedition. Such adventurous activities give opportunities to experience exposure to hardship and danger in peacetime, experience which is invaluable in our training for war.

Corporal Alan Chambers and Marine Charlie Paton trekking across the arctic plateau to reach the North Pole in 2000.

Chapter 11

International Terrorism – Worldwide Operations
2002–2012

"Everyone remembers where they were at the moment when the Twin Towers were attacked. I was on a hilltop in a Turkish training area with Brigadier Roger Lane on our way to Exercise SAIF SAREEA in Oman, huddled round a Clansman HF set listening to the world news. We immediately recognised its significance, both to world events and to our short-term programme, but no-one could have predicted the monumental impact it was to have on the Royal Marines in the years that followed."

Major General Gordon Messenger DSO* OBE

A s the new century unfolded with the devastating event of the terrorist attacks on New York and Washington on 11 September 2001, much of the world suddenly found itself at war with terrorism. Among the first troops to be involved were the Royal Marines, fortuitously on a major amphibious exercise in the Persian Gulf area. 40 and 45 Commandos with elements of other Corps units were soon deployed in Afghanistan, in operations against an enemy that was implicated in planning international terrorism. In November 2001, the SBS were the first formed body to enter the capital Kabul, followed by 40 Commando who established a presence in the city. By patrolling with the local police force they prepared the ground for the International Security Assistance Force (ISAF). Later they were joined by 45 Commando, who deployed on offensive operations (Operation JACANA), often carrying up to 100 pound loads, working at altitudes of thirteen thousand feet, in mountainous country near the border with Pakistan. After two initial contacts in which they were out-witted and out-gunned, the enemy proved to be very elusive. Amongst many finds of rockets, mortar and artillery ammunition, and arms, some twenty to thirty truckloads of munitions were found in a cave complex, and were destroyed in a controlled explosion of spectacular proportions, together with remaining terrorist installations and materiel.

The fact that recruits straight from Lympstone could join their units and deploy successfully directly into the mountains, into a challenging, hot, and very hostile environment, validated the Corps' rigorous basic training regime. On departure they could look with satisfaction on their achievement in denying the enemy vital ground and ammunition, and in bringing some stability to an area that had been traditionally rife with terrorism, crime and banditry.

Meanwhile, amongst many other operations, the SBS, working often with the Americans, became engaged in the rescue of a CIA agent from an Afghan prison revolt in which five hundred al-Quaeda and Taliban, many still armed, were held. For three days the SBS, in the Mazar-i-Sharif region, brought down heavy fire and aerial strikes to quell the revolt and help release the American captive.

Kuwait and Iraq

Following the allied liberation of Kuwait from the forces of Iraq in 1991, Saddam Hussein was required by the United Nations to disarm, and to declare and destroy his chemical, biological, and nuclear programmes. Despite his prevarication, obstruction and concealment over a number of years, the UN inspectors made some headway in discovering what weapons or materials existed, but in 1998 he expelled them. Later, in 2002, he reluctantly re-admitted them following a unanimous Security Council Resolution, but was unable to explain what had happened to the materials identified by the inspectors in 1998 (which included elements for producing chemical and bacteriological weapons). As Iraq failed to comply with the will of the United Nations, and based on the authority provided by a series of UN resolutions since 1991, the UK joined a US - led coalition that was prepared to use force as a last resort to secure Iraqi compliance. The overriding political objective was to disarm Saddam of his weapons of mass destruction, and to support the Iraqi people in their desire for peace, freedom and good government. Despite Security Council lack of consensus, coalition forces commenced operations against the regime on 20 March 2003, involving, eventually, some 46,000 service men and women, of which 3,000 were Royal Marines. The UK name for this operation was Operation TELIC.

In January and February that year 3 Commando Brigade (Brig Jim Dutton) had deployed to the Middle East and commenced training; the attachment of 15 Marine Expeditionary Unit USMC under command demonstrated the strength of our relationship with our American colleagues, and a squadron of their light tanks provided armoured support. At approximately 2000 hours on 20 March, 40 Commando led a helicopter assault to secure the area of an oil pipeline south of the town of Al Faw, with the objective of securing the oil facilities before they could be destroyed by the Iraqis. The first non-Special Forces to enter Iraq, they encountered light opposition from Iraqi irregulars, which they defeated, and despite being prepared for demolition, all objectives were secured without loss or destruction. The significance of this success should not be underestimated, given the ecological disaster that would have resulted had demolition taken place.

In the early hours of 21 March, 42 Commando landed, also by helicopter, on the Al Faw peninsula. Deploying to the north-west of 40 Commando, they established a blocking position to prevent enemy interference with 40 Commando's objectives. The Brigade Reconnaissance Force landed alongside 40

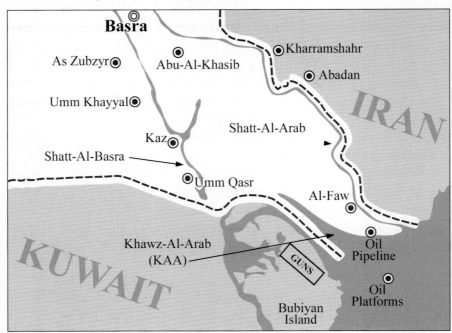

A Landing Craft Air Cushion (Light) of 539 Assault Squadron patrols the
Az Zubayr river near Umm Qasr.

Commando, but during their move a USMC CH-46 helicopter crashed in poor
visibility, killing all on board – these included five Royal Marines, three men
from 29 Commando Regiment Royal Artillery, and the USMC crew.

After securing its initial objectives, 40 Commando advanced towards Basra,
and over the next seventy-two hours came under repeated attack by Iraqi armour
on their approach to the city. With the help of a squadron of Challenger 2 tanks
from the Queen's Dragoon Guards and surveillance and offensive support from
Naval Air Squadrons, the Commando destroyed a full Iraqi Armoured Battle
Group. During this advance the Commando had to fight a twenty-hour battle
against an Iraqi battalion which they also defeated, thus allowing the advance
towards Basra. 42 Commando moved swiftly against opposition through Umm
Qasr to allow them to lead the 'break-in' battle to Basra. The Commando pushed
through more serious opposition to achieve its objectives, culminating in the
capture of Saddam Hussein's Basra Palace. After a brief period of consolidation
within the city, the Commando changed from a war role to a peace enforcement
task within a matter of hours. They then proceeded to defuse the local tensions
and co-ordinate the distribution of much needed humanitarian aid. The

Commando quickly reduced its confrontational posture, and the young Marine's ability to 'win friends and influence people' came to the fore. Although the ensuing football matches with the locals did little to increase the Corps' sporting prowess, it did help greatly in reducing tension and engendering trust.

45 Commando supplied individual reinforcements to Brigade units, and company groups who operated either on separate tasks, or under command of the Brigade as appropriate, while those left at home were on stand-by as firefighters during a period of industrial action by the fire service.

The new Landing Platform Dock, HMS Albion, during Exercise JOINT WINTER, 2004.

4, 9 and 539 Assault Squadrons employed their full complement of craft to support all sea-based phases of the conflict. Hovercraft, landing craft and raiding craft were all used to great effect during the initial amphibious assault and continued to have an impact in clearing and securing the marshlands of southern Iraq. The Commando Logistic Regiment not only supported the Brigade throughout, but also used its supplies to support 1 (UK) Armoured Division, proving the invaluable nature of stocks held afloat on amphibious shipping. The Royal Marines Reserve, in their first compulsory mobilisation, deployed 117 ranks who served alongside regular Royal Marines, displaying all the determination and commando spirit expected of them. The highest compliment that could be paid to these men was that they were indistinguishable from their regular brethren. The Royal Marines Band Service again also rose to the challenges put before them. The men and women provided continuous support in many forms, from medical and decontamination work, to morale boosting musical performances.

Iraq Again

In July 2004, 40 Commando deployed again to Iraq – this time to Shaibah, to the southwest of Basra, where they protected the oil installations, the economic mainstay of the country, whilst also fulfilling a variety of other roles – mobile patrols, convoy and force protection (with particular success in Baghdad), long range desert penetration, and training local forces. This last task would, it was hoped, eventually enable the Iraqi forces to take over responsibility for the security of their own country. As was becoming the norm, RM Reservists filled billets in the Commando, were employed in various Civilian-Military Co-operation roles (CIMIC), worked as watchkeepers in Divisional Headquarters, and assumed roles in the National Support Element.

A major preoccupation and a factor in operational readiness for the latter part of 2004 and much of 2005 was the introduction of new and complex equipment to the Brigade: The key item was the Bowman Communication and Information System. Much more than a new set of radios, this system brought the ability to transmit secure voice and data down to section level, with each individual in a rifle section having a personal radio. A thirteen-week conversion package for each Commando needed to be followed by exercises at Company, Unit and Brigade level before operational competence was achieved, with some thirty-nine Royal Navy warships, and 748 RM vehicles needing modification.

2005 saw a unique event – two Royal Marines Officers were knighted in The Queen's Birthday Honours List: Lieutenant General Sir Rob Fry KCB CBE and Lieutenant General Sir Robert Fulton KBE. These Officers reflected the ability of our senior ranks to compete successfully with the other services for the highest appointments both in the Ministry of Defence, and on international operations. General Fry took over as Deputy Commanding General, Multi-National Force Iraq, the following year, and General Fulton, following his last appointment as Deputy Chief of the Defence Staff (Equipment Capability), became the Governor of Gibraltar on his retirement in 2007. Also in 2005 Major General J B Dutton CBE, CGRM, with his COMUKAMPHIBFOR HQ, commanded the Multi-National Division (South-East) in Iraq. Major General

Andrew Salmon CMG, OBE commanded this same Multi-National Division (South-East) in 2008/9 and closed down the UK campaign in Iraq, so the Corps was first in to Iraq in 2003 and last out in 2009.

108 Viking All-Terrain Vehicles (Protected) entered service – the first armoured vehicle to be operated by the Corps since WW2 leading to the final designation of its operational unit as Armoured Support Group RM on 10 December 2007. Looking to Surface Manoeuvre capability, the Offshore Raiding Craft (ORC) was introduced, with the ability to provide an 'over the horizon' assault capability carrying a section of eight fully equipped men, or an array of craft mounted weapons systems in the fire support variant, while the first of the new Landing Ships Dock (Auxiliary), RFA Mounts Bay, arrived to replace the small and ageing Landing Ships Logistic, veterans of 1960s vintage. 539 Assault Squadron provided a Boat Group operating ORC, and Rigid and Inflatable Raiding Craft in support of the Army in Iraq.

Afghanistan Again – and Again.

In 2005 the NATO allies decided to expand the remit of ISAF to cover all the country, and the province of Helmand was allocated to UK. In 2006 elements from 40 and 42 Commandos deployed there for force protection duties, and to provide security for the bases being built. The Afghanistan deployments were titled Operation HERRICK, the name for the continuing operations that were to preoccupy UK's armed forces for the next decade. Following 16 Air Assault Brigade's tour, the bulk of the Commando Brigade deployed to Helmand Province in October 2006. On this (Operation HERRICK 5) and all future 3 Commando Brigade RM deployments 40 Commando remained behind, and took its turn in Afghanistan as a sub-unit of an Army Brigade: thus there was always an RM unit available in UK for contingency tasks, and to keep alive amphibious skills. The mission of the Brigade's Command Support Group was to form an Information Exploitation Group with three principal roles: reconnaissance in Southern Afghanistan, co-ordination of security, and finally reconstruction and development in the Province. 45 Commando operated from Camp Tombstone, working alongside the Afghan National Army to improve their professional standards.

Their new equipment was impressive, with Viking, Javelin anti-tank missiles,

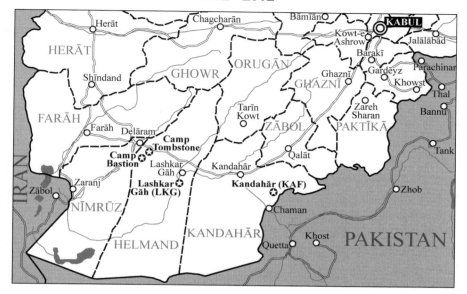

and close support from Army Apache attack helicopters and Harrier aircraft (some flown by Royal Marines); the Commando Battle Group packed a considerable punch. 42 Commando took over from 3rd Battalion, The Parachute Regiment in the desert of Helmand Province. They were based in the purpose-built Camp Bastion, but with elements occupying key installations in strategically important locations such as the Kajaki Dam and Sangin Town District Centre. From there numerous offensive operations against Taliban strongholds were launched, with the aim of providing a secure working environment for Non-Governmental organisations, and permitting attached Royal Engineers to rebuild local infrastructure such as hydroelectric plants. When conditions allowed, interaction at grassroots level was the primary aim, for example organising and conducting Shuras (meetings) with local village elders. However when faced with Taliban attempts to disrupt this process, the Unit quickly resumed a more aggressive posture, which resulted in numerous tactical successes.

At the start of the summer of 2006 HMS *Bulwark* was near Spain. Due to the 2006 Israel-Lebanon crisis, on 15 July 2006 she was ordered to divert to Lebanon and to support operations evacuating British citizens from the conflict area. On 20 July, she evacuated approximately 1,300 people from Beirut in the biggest British evacuation. Her organic assault squadron (4 Assault Squadron) played a full part in assisting the evacuees. On completion of her extended deployment the ship returned to the United Kingdom.

The Brigade's tour ended in March 2007, however so successful was the Viking that a seventy-five man strong RM Armoured Support Company remained in Afghanistan, providing two troops of this vehicle for the use of our successors.

A number of Band Service personnel took part in operations with the Brigade in Afghanistan, where they worked in both their primary and secondary roles assisting the Medical Squadron and other sub-units of the Commando Logistic Regiment, and providing musical entertainment, particularly over the Christmas period, as well as supporting the repatriation ceremonies for dead British Service personnel. For a period starting in April 2007 the Band Service also provided personnel from the UK to assist the Army in Cyprus, in order to release infantry soldiers for front line duties in Afghanistan and Iraq. Proving their versatility, they undertook guarding and patrolling duties, as well as performing a variety of musical engagements ranging from full concerts and marching displays, to jazz combinations and Corps of Drums displays.

In 2007 40 Commando (augmented by 77 RMR ranks) was deployed on Operation HERRICK 7 as part of 52 Infantry Brigade, while at the same time the Commandant General was the senior British rank in the multi-national HQ there, with elements of COMUKAMPHIBFOR staff. For 40 Commando, one of the key actions was participation in the NATO-Afghan Operation MAR KARARDAD to take the Taliban stronghold of Musa Qaleh. Lieutenant Nixon, B Company, describes his Company's approach to the town:

> "Within 500 metres the enemy engaged with accurate small arms fire and RPGs; with rounds bouncing off the Vikings and RPGs exploding all around the vehicles – all inside were thankful for the extra armour. The Vikings returned fire with everything they had: HMG 0.5s, and GPMGs emptied belt after belt into the enemy positions and the Taliban responded with an equal weight of fire. Assessing that this would only be a small pocket of Taliban and that we could outflank them, we cracked on".

This was another demanding tour, and progress was made in restoring stability to the region, but the price paid by the Commando was three men killed and twenty-five wounded.

A Band of the Royal Marine Light Infantry c.1895. *From a painting by Simkin.*

The Royal Marine Artillery c.1897. *From a painting by Simkin.*

45 Commando making the first helicopter assault, Port Said, 1956.
From a painting by Lane.

The Assault on Limbang, L Company, 42 Commando, 1962.
From the painting by Cuneo.

'The Dhala Patrol', 45 Commando, 1965. *From the painting by David Shepherd.*

'Commando Pick Up', Norway, 1979. *From a painting by Philip Marchington.*

42 Commando's assault on Mount Harriet, 1982. *From a painting by Peter Archer.*

'In the Afghan Mountains'. *From a painting by Marianne Gibson.*

The Massed Bands of the Royal Marines march down the Mall following Beat Retreat on Horse Guards Parade, London, on the occasion of the Captain General's birthday.

RM Band Collingwood perform at the Invictus Games in London 2014

Presentation of Colours to all three Commando units, Plymouth Hoe, 2001.
Here the new Colours of 42 Commando are consecrated.

Presentation of the Royal Marines Cadet Colour by the Captain General Royal Marines,
The Duke of Edinburgh KG, KT

A 42 Commando Troop Commander sends a situation report during an operation to clear buildings occupied by the Taliban in Afghanistan, 2007.

The four swords of Peace won by 40 Cdo RM between 1966 and 2018 are paraded following the presentation of the fourth sword in April 2019 at Norton Manor Barracks, the home of 40 Cdo RM, (Crown Copyright)

Viking All-Terrain Vehicles (Protected) of the Armoured Support Group in Norway. These vehicles give a considerable level of protection to a section, whilst being sufficiently light-weight to allow them to cross the most demanding terrain, and to swim if necessary.

42 Cdo Gp formed up on Exercise BLACK ALLIGATOR 15 in the Mojave Desert, USA

Between October 2008 and April 2009, the majority of the Brigade (Brigadier G Messenger DSO OBE) deployed on Operation HERRICK 9. During the tour the Brigade enabled encouraging progress to take root across Helmand Province and for the first time, the Afghanistan Government was able to start making a real impact in outlying districts. Reconstruction and training of both Afghan Army and Police were also major tasks. 45 Commando dominated the Upper Sangin Valley whilst 42 Commando acted as the regional reserve for Regional Command (South) undertaking numerous aviation assaults across the Region to disrupt Taliban supply lines and deny the Taliban the initiative.

Later that year, the Corps family dedicated the new RM Memorial Wall at CTCRM on 27 September 2009: the Wall records the names of all Royal Marines who have died on operations since 1 January 2000.

On 20 March 2010, the UK Landing Force Command Support Group was retitled as 30 Commando Information Exploitation Group RM to better reflect its role, recently developed in the combat conditions of Afghanistan. The unit title drew on the history of the WW2 30 Commando, a specialist naval intelligence collection unit. In June 2010, CGRM, as COMUKAMPHIBFOR, with his headquarters took over command of Operation ATALANTA, the European Union operation to combat piracy in the Indian Ocean. Pirate groups, operating in fast boats, and usually based in Somalia, were capturing ships, and holding their crews hostage pending the payment of large sums by the owners. The international economic costs in terms of increased insurance, payment of ransom, and delayed or lost cargoes were considerable. The Fleet Protection Group, whose primary role was protection of the national nuclear deterrent at Faslane, continued to deploy its Fleet Contingency Troop successfully disrupting this activity through detention of pirates, destruction of their vessels, and confiscation of equipment.

Lance Corporal Matthew Croucher RMR, serving with 40 Commando in Afghanistan, was awarded the George Cross for throwing himself on a grenade before it detonated. His courage prevented death or serious injury to the other members of his patrol. Seen here with his tattered rucksack which absorbed much of the blast.

43 Commando Fleet Protection Group anti-piracy operations.

In 2012 The Fleet Protection Group became part of 3 Commando Brigade, and was at the same time re-named 43 Commando Fleet Protection Group RM, providing a morale boost for those serving in it. This also emphasised its link with the original 43 Commando, via Comacchio Company (and later Comacchio Group) – a previous Unit title, which itself commemorated the famous 1945 battle in Italy following which Corporal Hunter was awarded a posthumous VC. Now a unit of over 700 ranks, larger than a Commando, it was commanded by a Colonel, with a wide range of tasks.

In 2011 the Brigade deployed on its fourth tour of duty in Afghanistan, becoming 'Task Force Helmand', with the headquarters commanding 6,555 troops, consisting of – in addition to its RM elements – a number of 7 Armoured Brigade units, as well as a Danish battalion and an Estonian company. Since 2008 the Army unit, First Battalion the Rifles had been an integral part of the Brigade. CTCRM Band provided thirty-nine ranks who operated in a wide range of roles, their principal one being provision of the Ambulance Response Troop at Camp Bastion, where some 2500 casualties passed through their hands. Operation HERRICK 14 came at a critical juncture in the UK's campaign in Afghanistan, with the Task Force charged with improving security for the people of Central Helmand by supporting the Afghan Government in preventing intimidation and violence. Social outreach programmes, education, medical and veterinary initiatives were supported while at the same time military activity ensured that hard won gains were held, and that pressure on the insurgency was relentless. The citation for the award of the Military Cross to Marine Mark Williams gives an idea of the intensity of one particular action:

Marine Williams displayed enormous strength of character, bravery and coolness of thought under intense enemy fire in order to rescue a severely wounded colleague from the killing area of a well-coordinated and effective insurgent ambush. Williams was deployed to Afghanistan as a Rifleman with Juliet Company 42 Commando RM; twenty-two-years old, this was his second tour of Afghanistan.

As part of a Battlegroup operation Juliet Company were inserted into the Loy Mandeh Wadi to disrupt insurgent activity. This area was a notable insurgent safe haven from which enemy fighters prosecuted offensive operations into the Protected Communities of Nad-e-Ali. Shortly after landing by helicopter, Juliet Company faced ferocious and prolonged insurgent attacks from all sides for two days, receiving accurate machine gun and 40 mm projected grenade fire from enemy positions within 300 metres of their location. Realising they were at risk of becoming pinned down in their patrol base, they pushed out a series of patrols to find and defeat the insurgents who were encircling them.

On 26 May 2011, Williams was involved in one of these patrols. Over a kilometre from the patrol base, and in temperatures in excess of forty- five degrees Celsius, his patrol observed a gathering outside a compound and momentarily identified an assault rifle. As his patrol moved forward to investigate, Lance Corporal Harvey was hit in the chest with machine gun fire from 200 metres away. Harvey was lying in open ground in the insurgent killing area, still under fire. In spite of the heavy weight of fire, Williams without hesitation and with no thought for his own safety ran into this killing area to rescue Harvey. Upon reaching his severely wounded colleague, Williams immediately gave him life-saving first aid; all the time continuing to receive accurate small arms fire from multiple positions. Williams then dragged his colleague over thirty metres to what he believed to be the relative safety of a compound wall to shield him from further fire. Here Williams continued to provide life-saving first aid, but again he came under effective insurgent fire from yet another firing point. Taking no notice of the extreme danger he was in, he continued to give life-saving first aid. With the casualty stabilised and whilst waiting for the helicopter, Williams picked up his weapon and returned to the fight; so fierce was the accurate and unrelenting fire from Williams and his team that the insurgents retreated. This allowed Harvey to be extracted to Camp Bastion, where the medical treatment administered by Williams was heralded as exemplary and no doubt saved Harvey's life as he had been losing significant amounts of blood.

The actions of Williams in the most difficult of circumstances were exceptional; especially given his rank and limited experience. Caught in the killing area of an insurgent ambush, he ignored the barrage of enemy fire, acted quickly and decisively and put his life at extreme risk by dashing across open ground, to save the life of a fellow Marine. His selflessness, valour, tenacity in the face of a determined enemy and live-saving first aid skills on that day were in the finest traditions of the Corps.

The challenge was immense and diverse and came at the cost of seven Royal Marines lives, and a further sixteen of the Task Force. The background to the later deployments to Afghanistan was the knowledge that NATO would withdraw from the country by the end of 2014, thus the emphasis was on the training of, and gradual hand-over of responsibility to the Afghan Army, police, and national authorities. Significantly, in July, responsibility for security in the city of Lashkar Gar was transferred to Afghan national forces.

Given the lengthy time taken to train up for Operation HERRICK deployments – up to a year – there was little respite from operations, with units starting on their training cycle within months of finishing their post tour leave.

Men from 11 Troop M Company 42 Commando clearing a compound in the villlage of Bariku, Afghanistan in an operation against the Taliban insurgents

The cost to the Corps was considerable with a total, up to the end of 2011, of 72 men dying in Iraq and Afghanistan, and 238 wounded – a significant proportion of which had life changing injuries.

In 2009 Hasler Company was established in HMS *Drake*, Plymouth, to manage the recovery, rehabilitation, and re-integration of the wounded. The staff in the Company work initially to help individuals, including sailors and some soldiers, recover from their injuries after release from hospital, then assist in their rehabilitation, and finally support them as they are reintegrated either back into a full time service environment, or into the wider civilian community: in 2012 some eighty men were being provided with bespoke individual recovery plans.

The Corps 'family', headed by a re-invigorated, flourishing and very active RMA, provided immense support, particularly in terms of fund raising activities. An example was the 'Commando 999' organisation, consisting of former Royal Marines who were serving in the UK emergency services, who aim to raise one million pounds by 2014. Corps funds were reorganised by grouping several small funds into the RM Charitable Trust Fund (RMCTF) on 1 April 2010. The

Progress in Afghanistan. Brigadier Ed Davis OBE hands over responsibility for security of the provincial capital, Lashkar Gah to the Afghan National Security Forces 20 July 2011, here shaking hands with General Hakim Angar, Helmand's Head of Police.

RMCTF in 2011 spent over £1 million on charitable grants to the Corps family.

The Mediterranean and Beyond

At the beginning of 2011 unrest in Tunisia led to the overthrow of the ruling regime, and this led to similar anti-government movements in other North African and Middle Eastern countries – the so called 'Arab Spring'. Anti-government protests began in Libya in February 2011, and the government reaction prompted a United Nations Resolution authorising 'all necessary measures' to protect civilians, with UK, USA and France starting a bombing campaign against pro-government forces. At this time HMS *Ocean*, with elements of 40 Commando embarked, was in the Mediterranean as part of the first deployment of the newly conceived Response Force Task Group (RFTG) – a fleet of RN and RFA ships that planned to undertake exercises in the Mediterranean and Middle East over the spring and summer. Exercise COUGAR became Operation ELLAMY, and HMS *Ocean* was utilized as a platform for launching attack helicopter strikes against Libyan forces, with the embarked force available to conduct non-combatant evacuation (NEO) operations, a task that the RM Protection Team in HMS *Cumberland* did indeed carry out. The planned exercises took place, notably in Cyprus, Saudi Arabia and the United Arab Emirates but at all times as the RFTG moved East, the presence of the embarked force gave the Government one of a range of options to intervene, particularly if a NEO was required. A similar RFTG deployment was planned for late 2012.-

Defence Cuts

Against a background of global financial crisis since 2008, the Strategic Defence and Security Review (SDSR) of 2010 brought reductions in the size and capability of the armed forces generally: the Corps was now only required to provide a Lead Commando Group at very high readiness, thus reducing the assets, equipment and finance that were required to keep the whole Brigade at this state. 24 Commando Engineer Regiment, which had evolved from 59 Independent Squadron Royal Engineers, was not to have the manpower or resources to bring it up to full strength. One of the four 'Bay' class LSD(A)s was also sold, only five years after entering service, with a LPD placed in reserve. Further cuts in the armed forces were announced in 2012, and the Corps –

Marine Mark Ormrod receives his campaign medal at the 40 Commando medals parade 2008. In 2007 he stepped on a buried landmine which resulted in the amputation of both his legs and his right arm.

remarkably unscathed until now – was ordered to plan on a reduction in size of some 600 personnel by 2015.

A significant percentage of Royal Marines have previously been Marine Cadets so it was fitting that the Corps was able to mark the singular honour extended by Her Majesty The Queen to the three arms of Marine Cadets (RM Volunteer Cadet Corps, Marine Detachments of the Sea Cadet Corps and Marine Detachments of the Combined Cadet Force) with an inauguration parade at CTCRM on 25 September 2011 when all 3 arms received the style of 'Royal Marines Cadets'.

In July and August 2012, several RM units contributed personnel to a large tri-service force providing security support to the London Olympic Games. In addition to individual access control, the Corps provided armed ORC from 539 Assault Squadron and LCVPs from 9 Assault Squadron as backup to the Metropolitan Police on the River Thames whilst HMS *Ocean* provided command, aviation and logistic support from a mooring off Greenwich.

French and British Marines exercise together in Corsica in 2012

Chapter 12

Global Challenges and Transformation
2013 - 2019

4 0 Cdo was the last commando unit to serve in Operation HERRICK. In total, the Corps suffered 56 men killed in action or died of wounds and 322 more were injured. The Corps had been active across all facets of the campaign and it was the RM Harrier pilots who were the first RM aircrew to serve in Afghanistan. In 2004 the Harrier Force was committed to Op HERRICK and four Royal Marines would fly the Harrier on operations in the province before the Force's withdrawal in June 2009. Captain Mike Carty, the fourth RM Harrier pilot to be trained, was actually on the ground as a Troop Commander with 45 Commando in Afghanistan in 2003 and then returned there as a Harrier pilot in 2009. Major Phil Kelly served on three flying tours in Afghanistan, Major Rob Fenwick one tour. Major Jim Dresner, as an exchange pilot with the USMC flying the AV8B Harrier, the American equivalent, also flew missions in Afghanistan. Concurrently, Major Darley was the first RM officer to fly a USMC Super Cobra helicopter during the conflict. Another RM officer who distinguished himself in the air over Afghanistan was Major Mark Hammond flying Chinook helicopters as an exchange officer with the RAF. He was awarded the Distinguished Flying Cross for his superior flying skills while operating in Helmand province. In early September 2006, Hammond flew a night rescue mission to extract a severely injured soldier from a forward operating base. On his first approach the aircraft came under sustained small arms and Rocket Propelled Grenade fire and his approach had to be aborted because the helicopter was badly damaged. He courageously returned to successfully complete the mission in a replacement aircraft with the added fire support of Apache and A-10 aircraft.

The end of this land campaign enabled the Corps to focus on the demands of delivering their mandated defence role - "to land and sustain a commando group of up to 1,800 personnel from the sea from a helicopter platform and protective vehicles, logistics and command and control support from specialist ships, including landing and command ships". The Response Force Task Group (RFTG) was the means through which this was achieved, there being a COUGAR deployment each year, the task group ranging further east each deployment. In 2013 for example, the RFTG exercised in Gibraltar, Albania, Turkey, Crete, Jordan, Saudi Arabia, UAE, Oman, Pakistan, India, Philippines and Singapore. The Corps adapted quickly to its more traditional role, amply demonstrated in December 2013 by J Coy 42 Cdo RM from the Lead Commando Group and the Band Service, embarked on HMS *Illustrious*, during Operation PATWIN when they provided humanitarian assistance to the Philippines after Typhoon Haiyan.

The 350th anniversary of the formation of the Corps in 2014 offered an opportunity to celebrate our distinctive history, as only the Corps can, with a unique combination of formal and physically challenging events, demonstrating the great versatility and spirit of the Royal Marines. 42 Cdo RM carried out London Duties, the first time a RM unit had done so since 1986, providing guards at all the royal residences and the Tower of London. This was followed by the Foundation Parade for HM Royal Marines Cadets, who for the first time paraded through London and received the RM Cadets Banner from the Captain General, HRH The Duke of Edinburgh KG KT. The culmination of the celebrations was the Freedom of the City of London Privilege March in July in which the whole Corps Family was represented. Operations continued in parallel, the most

43 Cdo FP Gp RM conduct live fire counter FIAC Training

Offshore Raiding Craft from 539 ASRM in the Arctic (Crown Copyright)

significant being Operation GRITROCK, the UK response to the ebola crisis in Sierra Leone for which the Corps provided riverine mobility and force protection to joint force medical teams. Similarly, the demand for the Corps' knowledge and expertise by countries in all regions of the world continued unabated with Short Term Training Teams deployed from the other Brigade units throughout the year providing specialist training and capacity building to allies.

2015 by no means saw a slackening off from the tempo of exercises and operations. The rebalancing of 3 Cdo Bde RM into an effective scalable Very High Readiness force continued apace, the visible symbol being the Response Force Task Group on its fifth deployment; modular and scalable – once again deployed forward to the Gulf and beyond as part of the Navy's commitment to providing Continuous Amphibious Readiness in the disorderly and chaotic environment which in 2015 promised to be the norm for some years to come. The migrant crisis in the Mediterranean provided considerable employment for the Corps. In April, elements of 45 Cdo, embarked on HMS *Bulwark*, took part in operation WEALD off the coast of Libya as part of the mission to rescue migrants risking the crossing from North Africa to southern Europe. In operation SILVAN, the Corps also provided support to the UK Border Force, as

Y Company 45 Cdo RM on exercise in Scotland during Exercise JOINT WARRIOR 15

part of the continuation of the European Union response to the crisis, providing protection to the Border Force crews rescuing migrants. This task has since been extended into 2018.

The positive outcome of the 2015 Security and Defence Review confirmed a commitment to spending on defence and the explicit retention of a RM Brigade with associated shipping and the introduction of the QE Class aircraft carriers showed a clear resolve by Government to properly resource Defence. It also showed a clear role for the Corps as part of the UK's response to global instability and insecurity. 2016 saw the emergence of the Special Purpose Task Group, as a response to the lack of amphibious platforms required to generate large scale amphibious task groups, combined with the geographical spread of possible crises. SPTGs were based principally on task-organised company groups, but remained scalable commensurate to the demands of the mission. The decision this year by the Prime Minister to lift the restriction on women serving in ground close combat roles from January 2019 presaged potentially historic changes to the Corps. Typically, the Corps embraced the challenge and offered a welcome to anyone able to meet the commando standards.

The National Security Review of 2017, which sought to redefine the needs of UK Defence, for some time threatened the amphibious capability. However, considerable lobbying and the visible impact of the Lead Commando Group's operations in the Caribbean and Dominica after Hurricanes Irma and Maria did much to reinforce the utility of amphibious forces.

40 Commando deployed with almost no notice in response to the September

2017 Caribbean disaster. The strongest and most sustained Atlantic Storm ever recorded, Hurricane Irma's path across the Caribbean Leeward Islands was devastating, causing unprecedented and catastrophic levels of damage and untold misery to an estimated 75,000 British Nationals. 40 Commando's ability to react and deploy rapidly into an uncertain and desperate situation, and without mission-critical equipment and supplies, enabled the arrest of a fast deteriorating and desperate situation in the UK Overseas Territories of Anguilla, British Virgin Islands and the Turks and Caicos Islands. With 59 Commando Squadron Royal Engineers attached, 40 Commando did all it could to locate and assist stricken communities, enable local authorities and aid agencies, restore and reinforce law and order and get essential services back up and running. For over a month, all ranks across the Unit tackled multiple challenges in its stride, absorbing uncomfortable levels of risk, innovating at every turn, and applying impeccable judgement at all times. Against the odds, their collective initiative, determination, compassion and courage brought relief and hope to the traumatised populations in a desperate situation.

A marine from 40 Cdo RM clearing debris during Op RUMAN

Notwithstanding the success of 40 Cdo Gp in the Caribbean, the impact of savings measure on the Navy resulted in the cancellation of overseas exercises and a demand for manpower savings as part of the Corps' contribution to rebalancing manpower across the RN. The Corps' response to this demand was reorganization under the banner of Project Sykes. 42 Cdo RM was re-roled as a maritime operations commando to assume the maritime interdiction capability from 43 Cdo FP Gp; the other two commandos retained their Lead Commando Group role and 43 Cdo RM was reconstituted to focus on protecting the National Deterrent.

Regimentally, the most significant event of 2017 was the succession of HRH The Duke of Edinburgh KG KT as Captain General by HRH The Prince Harry of Wales. A decision met with intense satisfaction and enthusiasm throughout the Corps Family.

Despite its commitments across the world, closer to home the commando units provided support during the severe winter storms of 2017/18 and, more significantly, 40 Cdo RM provided military assistance to the civil authorities when they supported the police and Defence scientists after the use of a chemical agent in Salisbury. After twenty years' distinguished service, HMS *Ocean* was decommissioned in 2018. However, despite the loss of such a capable amphibious ship, a Special Purpose Task Group (SPTG) sailed east conducting defence engagement in the Mediterranean and Middle East, joining other amphibious units to form an amphibious task group, participating in Exercise SAIF SAREEA 3 in Oman and then on into the Far East. The loss of the LPH capability was partially offset by the arrival in service of the new HMS *Queen Elizabeth* (and *Prince of Wales*) – not amphibious ships, but capable of providing tremendous amphibious support with their air groups promising the prospect of 'fifth-generation commandos' fighting alongside 'fifth-generation jets'.

In 2019, the quality of the individuals serving in the Corps remains very high. For example: seventy-three percent of those joining as recruits had the educational qualifications to be considered for officer selection; and the Corps, representing only four percent of Defence manpower provided forty-two percent of UK Special Forces, as well as a RM company in the Special Forces Support Group. It is of note that the Corps in 2018 had become twenty-seven percent of the Naval Service. The spread of Royal Marines throughout the Defence area has also been remarkable. In 2012 six RM officers were serving away from the Corps in the rank of major general or above in various posts in Defence, including a lieutenant general as Chief of Joint Operations in the Permanent Joint HQ. In 2018, four RM general officers were serving away from the Corps, including one as Vice Chief of the Defence Staff.

In 2019 the Corps continued to demonstrate its distinctive contribution to UK Defence when 40 Cdo RM was awarded a fourth Sword of Peace, this latest sword for their contribution to humanitarian and disaster relief operations in the Caribbean following Hurricanes Irma and Maria in 2018. The commando became the only major unit in the Armed Forces to hold four Swords of Peace. Looking ahead, the Corps is focussed on adapting organisations, equipment and concepts as part of the Future Commando Force as an integral part of the Royal Navy's response to an increasingly ambiguous international system. It is therefore perhaps unsurprising that in January 2019, a Minister of State for Defence declared that "today the Royal Marines are the UK's specialised commando force—an elite unit held at very high readiness and trained for worldwide rapid response. They can deal with a wide spectrum of threats and security challenges, and operate in often dangerous and extremely difficult circumstances, including amphibious operations, littoral strikes and humanitarian relief as well as specialist mountain and cold weather warfare and jungle counter-insurgency. When diplomacy fails, the Royal Marines provide Government with an impressive spectrum of hard-power options with which we can respond".

A Royal Marines Maritime Sniper Team

The Duke of Sussex KCVO ADC, who took over the appointment of Captain General Royal Marines 19 December 2017, talking to recruits on completion of their 30 miler.
Copyright Globe & Laurel

Senior Royal Marines Appointments

The Captain General

HRH The Prince Alfred, Duke of Edinburgh was appointed Honorary Colonel of the Royal Marines in 1882. After his death, HRH The Duke of Cornwall and York, later Prince of Wales, was appointed Colonel-in-Chief in 1901 and continued to hold the appointment when he ascended the throne as King George V. King George VI assumed the title when he came to the throne in 1936 and in 1948 changed the title to Captain General. Her Majesty Queen Elizabeth II, on the occasion of her coronation, appointed HRH The Prince Philip, Duke of Edinburgh, as Captain General Royal Marines on 1 June 1953. He wore the uniform of a Royal Marines general officer with the badges of rank of a field marshal (crossed batons on a wreath of laurel with a crown above). When The Duke of Edinburgh, aged 96, stood down from all formal duties following the Captain General's Parade at Buckingham Palace on 2 August 2017, Her Majesty approved the appointment of HRH The Prince Henry of Wales, subsequently the Duke of Sussex, as Captain General Royal Marines on 19 December 2017. Prince Harry wears the uniform of a Royal Marines general officer with the badges of rank of a colonel, in broad alignment with the honorary appointments of other younger members of The Royal Family. The only other British military units that have a Captain General are the Honourable Artillery Company and the Royal Regiment of Artillery. Both appointments are held by HM Queen Elizabeth II.

Honorary Colonel

His Majesty King Harald of Norway was appointed an Honorary Colonel in the Royal Marines by Her Majesty The Queen in 1981, when he was the Crown Prince. He wears the uniform and badges of rank of a Royal Marines colonel.

The Commandant General

An RM general officer is always appointed as Commandant General RM: this role is as a head of one of the four Naval Service Fighting Arms but with specific duties as the serving head of the Corps responsible for advising the First Sea Lord on RM matters. It does not carry any command function but is rather a ceremonial and 'tribal chief' role.

Colonels Commandant

These are honorary appointments, which are normally held for approximately four years. Those appointed are usually retired RM general officers or brigadiers, but senior officers of other services may also be appointed. RM officers may wear either the uniform and badges of their rank on retirement or, as in the case of officers from other services, a RM general officers' uniform with the badges of rank of a colonel.

Honorary Colonels Royal Marines Reserve

Each RMR unit has an honorary colonel, who wears the regimental uniform of their rank on retirement or the approved alternative, which is Corps uniform (i.e. uniform worn by lieutenant colonels RM and below) with colonels' badges of rank.

Colonel Commandant Royal Marines Cadets

The Colonel Commandant RM Cadets is an honorary appointment. The incumbent wears the regimental uniform of his rank on retirement or the approved alternative, which is an RM general staff uniform (i.e. uniform worn by RM brigadiers and colonels) with colonels' badges of rank.

Appendix B

Corps Memorable Dates

23 APRIL – THE RAID ON ZEEBRUGGE IN 1918. Towards the end of the First World War, the 4th Royal Marine Battalion landed on the Mole to enable the blocking of the entrance to the canal, which was being used by the Germans as a base for their submarines. Two Victoria Crosses were awarded to the Battalion and no other battalion has since been numbered '4th'.

28 APRIL – GALLIPOLI IN 1915. The Royal Marine Brigade landed on the peninsula as part of the expedition to drive up towards Constantinople during the First World War. Together with 1 RN Brigade, they bore the brunt of the Turkish attacks and displayed great resolution in this major amphibious operation.

6 JUNE – THE LANDINGS IN NORMANDY IN 1944. During the Second World War, over 17,500 Royal Marines took part in the largest amphibious operation in history. They crewed most of the minor landing craft, manned the guns in the supporting capital ships and provided an Armoured Support Group, beach clearance and control parties and engineers. Five Royal Marine Commandos landed during the assault phase.

7 JUNE – THE BATTLE OF BELLEISLE IN 1761. On this island off the coast of France, two battalions of Marines served with great distinction at this siege during the Seven Years War. The laurel wreath in the Corps insignia is believed to have been awarded in honour of this distinguished service.

14 JUNE – THE RECAPTURE OF THE FALKLAND ISLANDS IN 1982. The Royal Marines were involved in virtually every significant aspect of this successful campaign. The main landing was planned and executed by 3 Commando Brigade, with RM detachments in many ships of the Task Force and with all landing craft manned by Royal Marines.

17 JUNE – THE BATTLE OF BUNKER HILL IN 1775. During the American War of Independence, after two unsuccessful assaults up the steep hill, which failed to dislodge the rebels, the 1st Marines and the 47th Regiment were committed to the battle. They took the position, after which it was reported that the Marines' 'unshaken steadiness was conspicuous'.

24 JULY – THE CAPTURE OF GIBRALTAR IN 1704, in the War of the Spanish Succession, was carried out by a brigade of British and Dutch Marines, who after the surrender successfully held the fortress against repeated attacks. Granted for the capture and defence of the Rock, this is the only battle honour borne on the Colours.

21 OCTOBER – THE BATTLE OF TRAFALGAR IN 1805 was the most decisive sea fight in British history and in which 2,867 Royal Marines took part. In their traditional stations on the upper decks, they bore a brave and important part in Lord Nelson's success.

28 OCTOBER – THE BIRTH OF THE CORPS IN 1664 was when King Charles II sanctioned the formation of the first regiment formed specifically for service at sea. The yellow uniform of the Duke of York and Albany's Maritime Regiment of Foot is commemorated by the yellow stripe in the Corps colours. The Corps Birthday is regarded as the Corps Day and is marked appropriately to celebrate the birth of the Corps, to pay tribute to the Corps Family and to commemorate former comrades

1 NOVEMBER – THE ASSAULT ON WALCHEREN IN 1944, in which Royal Marines Commandos and support craft guns' crews successfully played a gallant and leading part, resulted in clearing the entrance to the River Scheldt, thereby re-opening the Port of Antwerp to Allied shipping after the invasion of the Continent during The Second World War.

Unit Memorable Dates

HQ 3 Commando Brigade RM

21 MAY – THE LANDINGS AT SAN CARLOS WATER, 1982. 3 Commando Brigade was the landing element of the amphibious task group ordered to recapture the Falkland Islands. Sound planning during the voyage south culminated in a successful Brigade night landing in the San Carlos region. The choice of this remote sheltered landing area enabled the landing force to withstand the constant air attack of the Argentine Air Force, and played a major part in ensuring the successful recapture of the islands.

30 Commando Information Exploitation Group RM

20 MARCH – OPERATIONS ON THE AL FAW PENINSULA, 2003. During 3 Commando Brigade operations to capture the Al Faw Peninsula in Iraq, the United Kingdom Landing Force Command Support Group (the previous name for the Unit) operations commenced some two weeks before the Brigade landings. It was tasked with achieving information dominance over the enemy through surveillance, reconnaissance, electronic warfare, the provision of communications and the protection of Headquarters. The bravery and ingenuity of its members helped ensure that the Brigade maintained dominance over the forces arrayed against it. It had a pivotal role in the success of the Al Faw landings and the subsequent break-out to Basra.

40 Commando RM

3 OCTOBER – THE LANDING AT TERMOLI IN 1943. 40 Commando was part of a small force which landed at the seaport town under cover of darkness on the Adriatic Coast of Italy and behind the German lines. Complete surprise was achieved and by 0800 hours the town had been captured.

20 MARCH – THE CLEARANCE OF THE AL FAW PENINSULA, 2003. During the liberation of Iraq 40 Commando RM mounted an amphibious helicopter assault and seized key oil infrastructure on the Al Faw peninsula. As the first conventional troops to cross into Iraq, the strategic significance of the operation

was immense. In a two-week period of intense operations, they cleared a large expanse of enemy held terrain, and defeated a major enemy stronghold on the periphery of Basra. Their role in the success of the coalition operation was crucial and profound.

42 Commando RM

31 JANUARY – THE BATTLE OF KANGAW IN 1945. In Burma, after two days of hand-to-hand fighting 42 Commando captured Hill 70. The unit was immediately subjected to heavy artillery fire and then, after a lull of several days and in spite of heavy casualties, beat off repeated Japanese counter attacks to successfully hold the position.

11/12 JUNE – THE ATTACK ON MOUNT HARRIET IN 1982 DURING THE FALKLANDS WAR was part of 3 Commando Brigade's main assault on the Argentine positions on the high ground overlooking Stanley. By moonlight and in freezing temperatures, the unit moved undetected through minefields to successfully surprise the enemy in their rear.

45 Commando RM

23 JANUARY – THE ATTACK ON MONTFORTERBEEK IN 1945. After hard fighting in bitterly cold weather during the campaign in North West Europe, the leading troops of the unit captured German positions holding up the advance through Holland. In spite of determined counter-attack and fierce hand-to-hand fighting the positions were held. It was for his bravery during this action that Lance Corporal H E Harden RAMC was posthumously awarded the Victoria Cross.

11/12 JUNE – THE ATTACK ON TWO SISTERS IN 1982 DURING THE FALKLANDS WAR was part of 3 Commando Brigade's main assault on the Argentine positions on the high ground overlooking Stanley. Bold reconnaissance by junior leaders had pin-pointed well equipped and dug-in Argentine positions. A silent night approach was made up the jagged, craggy rock formations, which after fierce hand-to-hand fighting culminated in the capture of the feature.

Appendices

Commando Logistic Regiment RM

22 MAY – THE LANDING AT AJAX BAY IN 1982. The support provided for the three weeks of the campaign from this area where they had landed, in adverse weather conditions and often under heavy air attack, was a battle winning factor of the Falklands War. This was entirely due to the skill, dedication and exceptional devotion of the various elements of the unit.

1 Assault Group RM
(including Operational Landing Craft Squadrons)

6 JUNE – THE LANDINGS IN NORMANDY IN 1944. In the assault on the German held French coast, Royal Marines manned the minor landing craft carrying the first and subsequent waves. For weeks after the initial assault they continued to ferry ashore men, vehicles and stores. Both afloat in landing craft and ashore in Naval beach parties, Royal Marines played a prominent and vital part in the invasion.

21 MAY – THE LANDINGS AT SAN CARLOS WATER IN 1982. At the start of the campaign in the Falklands, landing craft squadrons landed 3 Commando Brigade on to five separate beaches without loss. They continued to offload the logistics in deteriorating weather and under constant air attack. They later assisted in mine-sweeping duties, raiding and insertion tasks. The Task Force could not have achieved its objective without this invaluable contribution.

43 Commando Fleet Protection Group RM

2 APRIL – THE BATTLE OF COMACCHIO IN 1945. In Italy, 43 Commando, to whom the modern unit owes its origin, successfully achieved its objectives during a brigade attack against strong opposition, in which it crossed a river in inflatable dinghies under fire. Next day, whilst moving across open country, the unit met intense fire and the leading troop was pinned down in the open. For his gallantry in drawing the enemy's fire, thereby enabling his troop to move to cover, Corporal Tom Hunter was awarded a posthumous Victoria Cross.

Royal Marines Organisation 2019

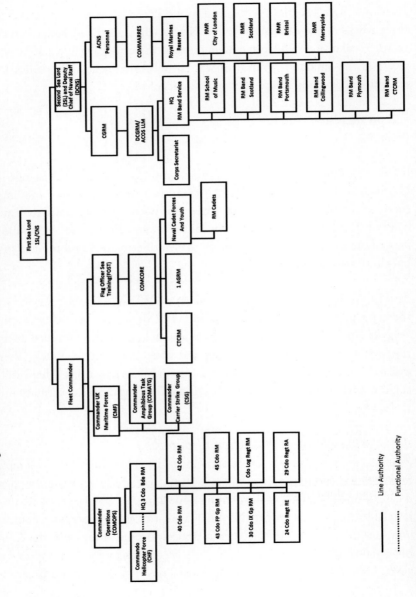

Line Authority
Functional Authority

Appendix D
Honours and Awards

	1854 – 1914*	World War 1	1919 – 1939	World War 2	1946-1993	1993 - 2012	2012 - 2018
Victoria Cross	4	5		1			
George Cross						2	1
GCB					1		
GCSI			1				
GCIE			1				
GCMG			2				
GCVO			1				
GBE		1					
KCB	7	3	7	2	15	3	2
KCMG		1			2		
KCVO				1	4		
KBE				2	1	1	
CB	16	25	18	10	41	7	6
CMG		314		1	2	3	
CIE				1			
CVO			1		3	1	
CBE		17	6	20	31	11	3
DSO	8	64(5)		33(4)	6(1)	7(1)	1
OBE		67	15	44	123	66	17
MVO	8		9		12	1	
MBE		11	13	84	130	210	31
Conspicuous Gallantry Cross						21	3
Distinguished Service Cross		36(1)		50(2)	5		1
Military Cross		57(2)		55(1)	33(2)	50	11
Distinguished Flying Cross					2	1	
Air Force Cross		2			2	1	
Albert Medal		2	3				
Distinguished Conduct Medal	16(2)	36			8	6	
Conspicuous Gallantry Medal	22	15		7			
George Medal				11	1	2	1
Distinguished service Medal		192	1	194(1)	8		
Military Medal		317(12)		105(1)	52(1)		
Distinguished Flying Medal					1		
Queen's Gallantry Medal					24	15	
Royal Victorian Order (silver/Bronze)	5		29		14	1	
British Empire Medal		3	7	99	324(1)	3	

*1854-1914 gallantry awards only
Bars to Awards shown in brackets

The George Cross

Colour Sergeant K H Haberfield
22 Nov 2005

The QUEEN has been graciously pleased to approve the award of the George Cross to the above mentioned for Services in the Field.

Lance Corporal M Croucher RMR
Afghanistan 9 February 2008

Lance Corporal Croucher has been awarded the civilian counterpart of the Victoria Cross, the highest gallantry award for civilians as well as for military personnel in actions which are not in the face of the enemy or for which purely military honours would not normally be granted.

In an act of great courage, and with complete disregard for his own safety, he threw himself on a grenade before it exploded, in order to safeguard the lives of the members of his patrol.

Lieutenant S J Shephard RM
3 Sep 2014

On 3 August 2013, Lieutenant Shephard Royal Marines was snorkelling in Egypt during a diving exercise when a fellow diver, who was also his friend, suffered an embolism and sank rapidly to the bottom. Shephard rescued his friend's body from a depth of approximately 60 metres. Shephard then led the ensuing evacuation, in the half light, over 200 metres of coral in bare and bloodied feet, providing continual emergency resuscitation until their arrival at the hospital. Unwavering throughout, he was focussed and extraordinarily composed during this most harrowing situation. Lieutenant Shephard showed truly exceptional courage and fortitude in his efforts to save the life of his friend. His unhesitating, selfless act, though ultimately unsuccessful, commands the highest national recognition.

Appendix E

The Victoria Cross

The following Royal Marines have been awarded the highest
British honour for gallantry:

CORPORAL J PRETTYJOHNS RM
The Battle of Inkerman, 5 November 1854. Successfully led a
section which dislodged Russian marksmen from some caves.

BOMBARDIER T WILKINSON RMA
The Siege of Sevastopol, 7 June 1855. Repaired damage to the
advanced battery's revetments under heavy fire.

LIEUTENANT G D DOWELL RMA
The Baltic, 13 July 1855.
Rescued the crew of a rocket boat under intense
'grape and musketry' fire.

CAPTAIN L S T HALLIDAY RMLI
The Siege of Peking, 24 June 1900.
Led the way into some burning Legation buildings under
heavy small arms fire.

LANCE CORPORAL W R PARKER RMLI
Gallipoli, 30 April 1915.
Displayed conspicuous bravery in rescuing wounded in
daylight under heavy fire.

MAJOR F J W HARVEY RMLI (*Posthumous*)
The Battle of Jutland, 31 May 1916.
Ordered the flooding of his turret's magazines although
mortally wounded, thereby saving his ship.

MAJOR F W LUMSDEN CB DSO*** RMA
France, 3 April 1917.
Led a party to recover six enemy guns while under heavy fire.

CAPTAIN E BAMFORD DSO RMLI
The Raid on Zeebrugge, 23 April 1918.
Led his company with initiative and daring in the face of
great difficulties (by ballot).

SERGEANT N A FINCH RMA
The Raid on Zeebrugge, 23 April 1918. Maintained
continuous covering fire from the exposed foretop, although
severely wounded (by ballot).

CORPORAL T P HUNTER RM (Posthumous)
The Battle of Comacchio, 3 April 1945. Advanced alone over
open ground to save his troop by offering himself as a target.

Appendix F

The King's Squad

On the occasion of his visit to the 4th Battalion in March 1918, preparing at Deal for their raid on Zeebrugge on St George's Day 1918, HM King George V also visited the Depot and witnessed recruit training. He was much impressed with what he saw and on completion directed that the senior squad of recruits under training should be designated 'The King's Squad'. As a mark of distinction it is customary for members of the Squad to wear a white lanyard on the left shoulder of their blue uniform and to wear the chinstrap of their cap 'down' below the chin. At one time one of the highlights of the Royal Tournament at Olympia and later Earl's Court was a drill display by the King's Squad of the Royal Marines. Today the senior recruit troop at the Commando Training Centre RM, Lympstone is titled 'The King's Squad'.

The King's Badge

Soon after his visit to Deal in 1918, HM The King further directed that the best recruit in the King's Squad should be awarded 'The King's Badge', "provided he reaches the required standard". The senior recruit receives his badge from the Inspecting Officer at the Squad's passing out parade. The gold wire embroidered badge, which consists of the cypher of King George V (GvR) within a laurel wreath, is worn at the top of the left sleeve. It is worn throughout his service in the Royal Marines, in all orders of dress no matter what rank he later attains.

The Prince's Badge

In 1978, to commemorate his 25th anniversary as Captain General, HRH The Prince Philip, Duke of Edinburgh directed that the best all-round musician or bugler completing training each year should be awarded the Prince's Badge. The silver wire embroidered badge, which consists of the cypher of HRH The Prince Philip surmounted by a coronet all within a lyre, is worn on the top of the left sleeve. It is worn throughout his or her service, in all orders of dress no matter what rank he or she later attains.

Appendix G

Freedoms and Privileges

The Royal Marines enjoy a number of privileges which were earned by their loyalty, devotion to duty and good character, they include:

Freedom of Cities and Towns

The freedom of a city or borough is the most honourable distinction a local government council can bestow. Regiments granted the Freedom of Cities and Towns invariably march through the area with their 'drums beating, bayonets fixed and colours flying' as a salute and a mark of respect to the citizens. The Royal Marines have been granted the freedom of:

Deal	1945	Medway	1979
Chatham	1949	Newcastle upon Tyne	1989
Plymouth	1955	Gibraltar	1996
Portsmouth	1959	The Wirral	1998
Poole	1973	Gosport	2005
Stanley, Falkland Islands	1976	Glasgow	2014
Exeter	1977	Birmingham	2018

Corps Civic Affiliation

In addition the Royal Marines have been affiliated to the town of Exmouth since 1968.

Civic Freedoms to RM Units

The following units have been granted the freedom of their local area:

The County of Angus	2003	45 Commando RM
The Borough of Taunton Deane	2003	40 Commando RM
The Town of Dartmouth	2003	RM Band BRNC
Dartmouth (disbanded in 2009)		
The City of Liverpool	2010	RMR Merseyside
The Town of Littlehampton	2013	30 Cdo IX Gp RM
The Town of Weston-Super-Mare	2014	40 Commando RM
The Borough of NE Lincolnshire	2015	45 Commando RM
The Borough of Wandsworth	2017	RMR City of London

Appendices

The City of London has the legal right to prevent troops freely entering the City. Since 1664 the Admiral's Regiment, and subsequently the Royal Marines, have been granted the privilege of marching through the City with drums beating, bayonets fixed and Colours flying. The origin of this privilege lies in recruits for the Duke of York and Albany's Maritime Regiment of Foot being found from the Trained Bands of London. The privilege is shared with only six other regiments, The Blues and Royals, Grenadier Guards, Coldstream Guards, The Princess of Wales's Royal Regiment, The Royal Regiment of Fusiliers and The Honourable Artillery Company. On 23 April 1974 the Royal Marines were affiliated to the Church of the Corporation of the City of London, St Lawrence Jewry.

RMR Merseyside receiving the Freedom of the City of Liverpool, 15 May 2010.

Appendix H

Associations with the City of London Livery Companies

The Worshipful Company of Stationers and Newspaper Makers adopted the Corps in March 1949, when Colonel Crosthwaite-Eyre MP suggested it to the then Master (Mr, later Sir Guy Harrison, a former regular Officer in the Corps). The Stationers' Trophy is awarded to the best trainee clerk or stores accountant who qualifies each year and the Cox Cup to the best student on IT/IS training courses each year at the Signals and Clerks Training Wing at the Commando Training Centre, Lympstone. The first Colours to be presented to 45 Commando RM are laid up in Stationers' Hall.

The Honourable Company of Master Mariners adopted the City of London Royal Marine Forces Volunteer Reserve (now RMR) in 1953. His Royal Highness The Prince Philip, Duke of Edinburgh, Captain General Royal Marines, is a Warden of the Court of the Master Mariners. Since 1964 the Commandant General has been an Honorary Member of the Company during his appointment.

The Worshipful Company of Musicians present a silver medal annually, which is awarded to the best student in the Bandmasters' Class at the RM School of Music. Another silver medal and a bronze medal, known as the Cassel Prizes, are awarded to the winner and runner-up in an annual competition for musicians under training at the RM School of Music. The Master of this Company for the year 1988/89 was Lieutenant Colonel Sir Vivian Dunn KCVO OBE FRAM RM, the first Principal Director of Music of the Royal Marines (1953–1966).

The Worshipful Company Of Armourers And Brasiers make an award to the best trainee armourer who qualifies each year.

Appendices

The Worshipful Company Of Plaisterers present prizes to the best students on the S1 (Signaller First Class) and LC1 (Landing Craft First Class) Courses each year. CGRM is elected by the Court of Assistants of the Company to Honorary Membership of the Company for the duration of his appointment. Retired RM Officers may also join the Company upon application to the Clerk. In 1983 the Company presented to the Corps a painting of the P&O liner 'SS Canberra' and LCU(9) in San Carlos Bay during the 1982 Falklands Campaign. This is now in the Officers' Mess at CTCRM Lympstone.

RM Colonels Commandant Biennial Lunch with the Captain General at Stationers' Hall on 7 November 2012. Note the stand of 45 Commando RM Colours laid up at the hall on 18 November 1969.

Appendix I

Associations with Other Marine Corps

The Royal Marines have particularly close associations with the Following Marine Corps of other countries.

The Royal Netherlands Marine Corps

Formed in 1665, during the Anglo-Dutch Wars, the Dutch Marines distinguished themselves both at sea and in raids on the English coast, where it is likely that they met their British counterparts. During the War of the Spanish Succession, when the two countries were allies, it was a combined force of British and Dutch Marines, under Prince George of Hesse-Darmstadt, which captured Gibraltar in 1704.

Today the Royal Netherlands Marine Corps, the Korps Mariniers, is an amphibious force with similar functions to the Royal Marines. It provides two companies and a Boat Group in the Netherlands Antilles, in addition to its major commitment with the United Kingdom/Netherlands Landing Force, with which it deploys a further Marine Battalion, a Special Boats Section and a Landing Craft Detachment. 1 (NL) Mortar Battery is often grouped under 29 Commando Regiment RA. This integration and cooperation, unique in NATO, was seen in 1991 during operations in Eastern Turkey and Northern Iraq.

The motto QUA PATET ORBIS (Wherever the World Extends) symbolises the service of the Corps throughout the world during its long history. A greetings message is sent to the RNLMC, the senior corps in the Netherlands armed forces, on the occasion of its birthday each year, 10 December.

The United States Marine Corps

In 1740, during Britain's war with Spain, a regiment of Marines was raised in the American colonies and accompanied 6 regiments of British Marines

on an expedition against important Spanish bases in the West Indies. Commanded by Colonel Gooch, a Virginian, the Regiment became known as Gooch's Marines. The expedition successfully accomplished its mission and the colonial Marines were credited with having rendered brave and gallant service against the Spanish.

During the Seven Years War thousands of Americans fought for the British cause. Colonial privateers, most of them carrying detachments of Marines, roamed the seas and aided British forces in dominating French sea power.

In the autumn of 1775, George Washington ordered the out-fitting of several vessels of war; each vessel carried a detachment of Continental Marines. On 10 November 1775, the Second Continental Congress resolved that two battalions of Marines be raised to serve during the American War of Independence. The date of this resolution is recognized as the birthday of the Marine Corps.

The USMC and the RM have served together on a number of occasions. During the Boxer Rebellion in China in 1900, when the senior USMC Officer was wounded, the combined Marine guards from the British and the US legations at Peking were commanded by Captain L S T Halliday RMLI, while both Corps were together in the relief column. From 1950 to 1952, during the Korean War, 41 (Independent) Commando RM served with great distinction under the command of the 1st US Marine Division. For their part in the fighting at the Chosin Reservoir, the unit was awarded the United States Presidential Unit Citation, denoted by a battle streamer borne on the Regimental Colour.

In 1929 the USMC presented a sports trophy to the RM. The presentation was made by Captain Gene Tunney, USMC (retired), the Heavyweight Boxing Champion of the World at the time. The trophy, now popularly known as the Tunney Cup, is competed for annually by RM units playing association football.

Today the association between the USMC and the RM continues with a number of Officers and NCOs being cross-posted between the two Corps and attending each other's courses, while the Commandant of the Marine Corps and CGRM have a regular exchange of visits, and a message of greetings is sent on 10 November each year, the birthday of the USMC.

The emblem of the USMC includes an eagle representing service to the nation, an anchor representing sea service, and also includes a globe representing worldwide service, but depicts the Western Hemisphere.

In 2019, more than 250 Royal Marines travelled to the east coast of the USA to compete for the Virginia Gauntlet trophy. Royal Marines competed in 19 different sports against the United States Marine Corps.(Crown Copyright)

Appendix J

Associations with Other Regiments

The Royal Marines have particular associations with the following Regiments:

The Princess of Wales's Royal Regiment
(Queen's and Royal Hampshire)

The Princess of Wales's Royal Regiment was formed by an amalgamation of a number of regiments which included the Queen's Royal Regiment (West Surrey) and the East Surrey Regiment. Although both Surrey regiments served as Marines during their early history, the Royal Marines particular connection was with the East Surreys. This was founded on a disaster in 1825 which befell half the regiment whilst on passage to India. Fire broke out in their ship during a violent gale in the Bay of Biscay and after abandoning ship the survivors, including many women and children, were transported to Chatham where they were befriended by the Royal Marines. Today officers and warrant officers class 1 of the Princess of Wales's Royal Regiment wear a blue lanyard, a custom which originated in the East Surrey Regiment. A message of greetings is sent to the 1st Battalion each year on the anniversary of the Battle of the Glorious First of June in 1794, when the Queen's Royal Regiment (West Surrey) were embarked in ships of the Royal Navy.

The Royal Regiment of Scotland

The Royal Regiment of Scotland was formed in 2006 by the amalgamation of six Scottish regiments, including the Argyll and Sutherland Highlanders with which the Corps enjoyed a long-standing bond of friendship. Early connections date from Balaclava in the Crimean War and Lucknow during the Indian Mutiny, but the main association stems from The Second World War. In July 1940, after the fall of Dunkirk, the 8th

Battalion, Argyll and Sutherland Highlanders served with the Royal Marine Brigade for over a year. When HMS Prince of Wales and Repulse were sunk in December 1941, the Royal Marines survivors joined up with the remnants of the 2nd Battalion, in the defence of Singapore. They formed what became known as 'The Plymouth Argylls', after the association football team, since both ships were Plymouth manned. Most of the Highlanders and Marines who survived the bitter fighting were taken prisoner by the Japanese. The Royal Marines inter-unit rugby football trophy is the 'Argyll Bowl', presented to the Corps by the Regiment in 1947. In 2017, to mark the 75th anniversary of the defence of Singapore and the 70th anniversary of the Bond of Friendship with the Argyll and Sutherland Highlanders, this association was extended to the Royal Regiment of Scotland with which personnel exchanges continue.

Australian Army

The Royal New South Wales Regiment and the 1st Commando Regiment

Elements of the predecessors of the Royal New South Wales Regiment served alongside the Royal Marine Battalion in the Sudan Campaign in 1885. Members of the Regiment were at Gallipoli and in France. In the Second World War a great many Officers and men served with distinction side by side with Royal Marines units in Crete in 1941. Independent companies were raised in Australia in 1941 and carried out commando training. Although these units were disbanded after the war, two commando companies were later reformed and one of these was enlarged and re-designated the 1st Infantry Battalion (Commando) (The City of Sydney's Own Regiment). The Royal Marines were closely connected with the training of officers and NCOs for these units and in 1960 HM The Queen approved alliances between the Corps and the 1st Infantry Battalion (Commando) and between 45 Commando RM and the 2nd Commando Company. A new alliance was approved later with the Royal New South Wales Regiment, and this has been extended to 1 Commando Regiment also. Annual greetings messages are sent on 6 March, the anniversary of the commencement of commando training in Australia in 1941.

Appendix J

Barbados Defence Force

Close links have existed between the Royal Marines and the Barbados Defence Force since 1985 when a bond was established following a series of cross-training exercises in the Caribbean. The alliance was approved by HM The Queen in 1992 and confirmed at a ceremony on 14th August 1993 in Bridgetown, Barbados, attended by the Commandant General. Annual greetings are exchanged on the anniversary of the parade.

France

The 9th Marine Infantry Brigade –
9eme Brigade D'infanterie De Marine

The 9eme Brigade D'Infanterie De Marine (9e BIMa) is part of France's Force d'Action Rapide (FAR). This Army formation is equipped as a light armoured brigade and has an amphibious role while maintaining an airmobile operations capability. The Brigade has personnel widely deployed throughout the world, particularly in former French colonies in Africa, and is at a high state of readiness for operations. The British and French Governments are committed to establishing closer links between their Armed Forces. On 16 February 1995, a 'Twinning Agreement 1895' (sic) was signed between 9e BIMa and 3 Commando Brigade Royal Marines to promote closer liaison between the formations, which have complementary capabilities. As a result of these closer links, regular exchanges of personnel occur between the two formations. This is combined with an increased incidence of both observing and participating in each other's exercises (at sub-unit level) and professional amphibious training courses. The partnership was reinvigorated in 2011 after the signing of the 2010 Lancaster House Treaty. This committed the two armed forces to greater interoperability, particularly with a view to creating a Combined Joint Expeditionary Force. This force has at its core both airmobile and amphibious capabilities. Consequently, the relationship between 9 BIMa and 3 Cdo Bde RM was re-invigorated with an ambitious set of bilateral activities which led to the validation of the CJEF in 2016.

Regimental Music

Quick March

A Life on the Ocean Wave was originally written as a song with words by Henry Russell in 1868. It was based upon a tune by an American, Henry Epps Sargent. J A Kappey, Bandmaster of the Chatham Divisional Band, arranged the tune as a divisional march, introducing part of the Naval song The Sea as the trio. In response to an instruction that all four Divisional Bandmasters should provide a march, one of which would be selected as the Regimental Quick March of the Royal Marines, Kappey submitted this arrangement. *A Life on the Ocean Wave* was successful and the War Office officially recognised it in 1882, the Lords of the Admiralty similarly recognised it in 1920 and the Royal Navy followed suit in 1927. Whilst Kappey's arrangement is the Official version, another very good arrangement was made in 1944 by Major F J Ricketts, the Director of Music of the Plymouth Division, better known as the composer, Kenneth Alford. A third arrangement was made by WO1 M McDermott in 1997.

> *A life on the ocean wave,*
> *A home on the rolling deep,*
> *Where the scatter'd waters rave*
> *And the winds their revels keep.*
> *Like an eagle caged, I pine*
> *On this dull unchanging shore;*
> *Oh give me the flashing brine,*
> *The spray and the tempest's roar.*

Slow March

A score of *The Preobrajensky March* was presented to the Corps in Tercentenary Year 1964 by Earl, later Lord, Mountbatten of Burma whose uncle, the Grand Duke Sergius, at one time commanded the Russian Preobrajensky Guards. The original composer of the march remains in doubt with evidence supporting two candidates, Ferdinand Hasse and Ernest Donajowski. Earl Mountbatten was given his score by King Alfonso of Spain in the late 1930s. The score was arranged by Lieutenant Colonel F V Dunn and the march was officially recognised as the

Appendices

Regimental Slow March of the Royal Marines on 10 June 1964. The arranger retired in 1968 and almost immediately became Lieutenant Colonel Sir Vivian Dunn KCVO OBE FRAM RM, the only Director of Music in any Service to be knighted.

Commando March

In addition to the Regimental Quick March, Commando units may use *Sarie Marais*, an old South African trekking song much used by the Boer Commandos. The song was written as a march by Toonsetting and then arranged by Captain F V Dunn in 1937. It has been reported that 3 Commando Brigade officially adopted the march, arranged by the Brigade's Bandmaster Dixon, in 1948. Captain Dunn's arrangement was officially adopted by the Corps on the 28th August 1952.

> *O take me back to the Old Transvaal*
> *That's where I long to be,*
> *I left my little Sarie where the mealies grow*
> *Just by the green thorn tree.*
> *And there I'll be to meet her where*
> *I loved her so*
> *Down by the green thorn tree.*

Commando Logistics Regiment

Army and Marine, written by Zehle and arranged by Hewitt, was first played as the adopted Regimental March at the Regiment's inaugural parade on the 11th June 1972.

Inspection Music

The Globe and Laurel. This march was the regimental slow march until 1964. It is an arrangement by Vivian Dunn of the traditional old English Air, *Early One Morning*, which he composed in 1935 for ceremonial use when the Royal Marines first carried out Public duties in London.

Salutes

These vary according to the rank, appointment or position of the recipient. *The National Anthem* is played in full for the Sovereign whilst other members of the Royal Family receive the first six bars only. *Rule Britannia* is the General Salute for admirals and commanders-in-chief whilst other flag officers receive Iolanthe. The General Salute for Governors is *Garb of Auld Gaul*. Unit commanding officers and VIPs, excepting flag officers, receive the bugle call *Alert* followed by drum ruffles and the call *Carry On*. These salutes have been in use since 1927 until, in 1988, the first eight bars of *Preobrajensky* (played in quick time) was added as the salute for Royal Marine general officers.

Advance in Review Order

The Royal Marines use the Army's *British Grenadiers*.

Massed bands march up the Mall 2009 (© *Les Scriver*).

Nicknames & Sayings

Jollies

This was the nickname of the Trained Bands of the City of London, who provided many of the recruits for the first regiment formed for service at sea. It is a term seldom used today but is to be found in Rudyard Kipling's famous poem *Soldier an 'Sailor too* and Kenneth Alford's well known march composition *H M Jollies*. At one time a Royal Marine was often called 'Joey', although the term eventually died out, the subaltern of a ship's RM detachment was usually referred to as 'Young Joe', whilst the Officer commanding the detachment was always 'Major', and the senior NCO was known as 'Sergeant Major', regardless of his rank.

Royal

Naval mess-deck slang for a Royal Marine. Naval Officers normally referred to their RM counterparts as 'Soldier'. A plausible explanation for this nickname, for which there is absolutely no supporting evidence, is as follows. After 1802, when the Corps was designated 'Royal Marines', Marines would, as a point of pride, refuse to answer if a sailor called out "Hey Marine, give us a hand". On the other hand they would usually respond willingly if addressed as 'Royal Marine'. The shortened style of 'Royal' quickly became the accepted nickname.

Lobsters

A very old nickname for a soldier because of their scarlet tunics. The RMLI, known as 'The Red Marines', were therefore 'Lobsters', whilst the RMA, 'The Blue Marines' were *'Unboiled Lobsters'*, all terms seldom heard today. Bluejackets also used to call Marines 'Turkeys'.

Bootneck

A term deriving its origins from the leather 'stock' worn round the neck inside the collar by soldiers. Sailors goaded Marines by saying 'Take my sea boots off your neck', implying that a piece had been cut from his boots to serve as a stock. The expression is now used widely to mean a Royal Marine.

Leatherneck

A term having the same origin as 'Bootneck' but normally applied to a United States Marine and it is the title of their monthly magazine.

Dead Marine

Means an empty wine bottle. Lieutenant Colonel W P Drury RMLI, a noted writer of naval stories and playwright, relates that the Duke of Clarence used the expression at a dinner party and when a Colonel of Marines looked annoyed, the future King William IV explained that 'He has done his duty once, and is ready to do it again'.

Tell It To The Marines

Often used with a sneer, as though it meant that only a Marine would be credulous enough to believe it. Colonel Drury wrote on the contrary that it was a test of truth as Marines, who served all over the world could verify or belie any 'wild' story. Sir Walter Scott used the expression in *Red Gauntlet* (1824) and Lord Byron in *The Island* (1823).

Horse Marines

An expression giving an idea of incongruity, from the absurd thought of mounted men on board ship. Nevertheless over the years Marines have often carried out mounted duties ashore. However the term is likely to have originated from two troops of the 17th Light Dragoons (now the Queen's Royal Lancers) which served afloat in HMS *Success* in the West Indies in 1795, but whether in fact they acted as Marines is not known.

Appendix M

The Royal Marines Museum

The The Royal Marines Museum (RMM) is a subsidiary charitable company limited by guarantee of the National Museum of the Royal Navy (NMRN). It also has the status of a recognized Corps agency. The RMM tells the stories of the Royal Marines past and present with a vast collection of objects, paintings and archive documents and thus plays a major role in preserving Corps history. The collection contains over a million photographs, a million documents and 30,000 objects plus over 8000 medals including all the ten Victoria Crosses won by members of the Corps. Originally housed in the former Officers' Mess of the Royal Marine Artillery, the museum's public galleries closed in 2017 as part of a project to move the collection into a new site in Portsmouth Historic Dockyard. Today, an element of the collection remains on display in the Historic Dockyard while the collection is moved and new premises and storage prepared. The attractive grounds of the former museum incorporate a peaceful Garden of Remembrance containing a wide range of memorials which remain open to the public. The "Yomper" statue, recalling the photograph of Corporal Peter Robinson marching across East Falkland, remains overlooking the Solent.

The Corps of Drums in front of the Yomper commemorating the departure of the final Corps agency, the Royal Marines Historical Society, from the former RM Museum at Eastney in January 2019

Customs & Corps Colours

The King's Candlesticks

On 21 December 1949, not long after his title changed from Colonel-in-Chief to Captain General Royal Marines, HM King George VI presided at a dinner of the Officers of the Corps at the Savoy Hotel, London. For the occasion, each Royal Marines Officers' Mess provided a pair of candelabra. The candles were lit just before the Loyal Toast. His Majesty expressed a wish that, in future at formal dinners, after the table had been cleared and the port passed, other lighting should be dimmed and the King's Candles lit in what is an exclusive ceremony to the Royal Marines.

The Loyal Toast

On 23 July 1964, to mark the Tercentenary of the formation of the Admiral's Regiment, HM Queen Elizabeth II dined with the officers of the Royal Marines. The dinner, at which HRH The Duke of Edinburgh, as Captain General,

Royal Marines Officers at the 2012 Corps Dinner on 24 October 2012 stand as the Regimental March *'A Life on the Ocean Wave'* is played after dinner.

Appendices

presided, was held at the Royal Naval College, Greenwich. It was on this occasion that, at the instigation of Admiral of the Fleet, the Earl Mountbatten of Burma (then Chief of the Defence Staff and the following year to be appointed a Colonel Commandant Royal Marines), Her Majesty granted the Royal Marines the privilege of drinking the Loyal Toast seated when in their own messes. This privilege extends also to the Sergeants' Messes and those of Junior Non-Commissioned Officers.

Toast to the Captain General
Immediately following the Loyal Toast, the President proposes the toast to the Captain General. This toast is also drunk seated.

Corps Colours
The significance, proportion and sequence when worn horizontally is:

Blue (Navy Blue): The Corps' status as a constituent part of the Naval Service – 8 parts (sometimes authorized to be reduced to 4 parts).

Yellow (Old Gold): The coat colour in 1664 – 1 part.

Green (Light Infantry Green): Perpetuates Light Infantry title – 1 part.

Red (Drummer Red): The infantry tunic colour until 1876 – 2 parts.

Blue (Navy Blue): The Corps' status as a constituent part of the Naval Service – 8 parts (sometimes authorized to be reduced to 4 parts).

Specialist Qualification Badges

Pilot

Air crewman

Special Forces
Parachutist

Parachutist

Special Forces
Communicator
Parachutist

Sniper

Bugler

Musician

Tradesman*

Telecommunications
Technician

Medical
Assistant

*Tradesmen include: Vehicle Mechanic,
Artificer Vehicle, Armourer and Metal smith

Classes in all the qualifications below are donated by:
1st Class – a crown above the badge
2nd Class – a star above and a star below the badge
3rd Class – a star above the badge

Drill/Platoon
Weapons

Communications
Technician

Drivers

Letter in wreath donates:
AE – Assault Engineer
AS – Armoured Support
C – Clerk
CI – Combat Intelligence
HW – Heavy Weapons
IS – Information Systems
K – Chef
LC – Landing Craft
ML – Mountain Leader
MP – Military Police
SA – Stores Accountant
SC – Swimmer Canoeist

Physical
Training

Signallers

HUMINT

Lanyards

Coloured lanyards are worn on the right shoulder of Lovat and tropical stone uniforms including shirt sleeve order by all personnel serving in operational or predominantly operational units, as listed below. These lanyards are not worn in blue or tropical white uniform, mess dress or on combat or training dress.

Green...Headquarters 3 Commando Brigade RM
Old Gold and Scarlet.......................43 Commando Fleet Protection Group RM
Navy Blue..Commando Logistic Regiment RM
Navy Blue and Light Blue...Commando Helicopter Force
Light Blue...40 Commando RM
White..42 Commando RM
Red..45 Commando RM
Green, Light Blue and Black...Special Boat Service
Sand and Green..................30 Commando Information Exploitation Group RM
Old Gold and Rifle Green...............................539 Assault Squadron RM
Navy Blue and Scarlet..1 Assault Group RM
(including Ships' Assault Squadrons)

All officers and WO1s wear a navy blue lanyard on the left shoulder in Blue, Lovat and Tropical Stone uniforms including shirt sleeve order but not in Tropical White, Mess or Combat Dress.

Recruits in the King's Squad (see Page 149) by custom wear a white double cord lanyard on the left shoulder in Blue uniform.

Appendix Q

The Green Beret

During the early days of Commandos, ranks continued to wear their own regimental headdress and cap badge. There were seventy-nine different badges being worn in No 1 Commando alone! In 1942, the officers of this Commando decided that matters should be regularised and that a beret would be most practicable. The Royal Tank Regiment had worn a black beret for many years and the recently formed Parachute Regiment had chosen a maroon beret. No 1 Commando wore a flash on their arm depicting a green salamander going through fire, which gave a choice between green, red and yellow. Green was deemed to be the most suitable. Their submission to the Chief of Combined Operations was forwarded by Lord Mountbatten to the Under-Secretary of State for War in a letter of 1 May 1942 and the first issue to Royal Marines Commandos was made in October that year. A local firm of tam-o-shanter makers in Irvine (Ayrshire) produced a beret made from some green cloth of the colour still worn today.

© Crown Copyright.

Appendix R

RMA – The Royal Marines Charity

Giving a lifetime of support to the Royal Marines Family

RMA – The Royal Marines Charity was formed on 1 April 2019 from a merger of the Corps' membership association, the Royal Marines Association (RMA), and its fundraising charity The Royal Marines Charity (TRMC).

The RMA was established in early 1946 to maintain cohesion and contact amongst Royal Marines demobilised after WWII and to help them find employment, aims which endure today. Latterly, with TRMC's financial backing, the RMA also delivered welfare support to members of the Corps Family who found themselves in need.

TRMC was established as the RM Charitable Trust Fund in 2010 to help the wounded, injured and sick resulting from operations in Afghanistan and Iraq, and merged with The C Group in 2016 to incorporate an employment support function for those medically discharged, creating TRMC.

In response to calls from successive CGRMs who challenged the charities to improve support to the whole Corps Family, and with the modernisation of the RMA that began in 2008, both charities found their roles in the support they provided to the Corps family were overlapping. This resulted in inefficiencies in the delivery of support to beneficiaries, with inevitable duplication of effort and confusion amongst beneficiaries and benefactors.

Thus the merged charity brings a number of significant advantages to the whole Royal Marines community - serving, retired and families:

- Maximises use of whole Corps Family concept as a single network for comradeship, benevolence, heritage, transition and amenities.
- Provides a clear single point of entry for support.
- Allows cost-efficiency and sustainability.
- Enables improved operational resilience.
- Ensures greater clarity of message and brand.
- Delivers greater total impact than 2 stand-alone charities
- Provides improved transparency and effectiveness of delivery
- Removes misperception of competition.
- Enhances RMA membership activities and events

RMA-The Royal Marines Charity's mission is to provide support, advice and friendship to serving and retired Royal Marines, their families, those who aspire to join and those with close links to our Corps; to sustain and promote the Royal Marines' traditions and esprit de corps, and to generate funds, non-financial benefits and access to employment in order to provide the best possible through-life charitable support.

In February 2019, membership was growing rapidly, with 12,658 members, of which 3,623 were serving Royal Marines. There were 98 Branches in the UK and overseas, organised into 7 regions. In addition to local branches, which have traditionally been the bedrock of the RMA, a number of special interest Branches had been established ranging from RMA Cycling, through the RMA Concert Band to RMA Riders and RMA Rugby. Membership events are run throughout the country to enhance comradeship.

The Charity supports activities at CTCRM by providing mentors for every recruit troop throughout its training, outside the rigours of the formal training process to give advice, a friendly ear and encouragement. Funding is provided to ensure Aggie's pastoral workers are able to support families in addition to recruits.

In addition, a large number of fundraising events are run across the UK and occasionally overseas in pursuit of its aim to raise £3m each year to meet the needs of the Corps family. The Charity runs purely on donations; of every £1 raised in 2017, 93p were directed into charitable support.

The main focus is the provision of welfare support to those who find themselves in need, in such areas as mental or physical health challenges, financial or relationship difficulties, or maintaining independence in old age.

RMA-The Royal Marines Charity works closely with partner charities and organisations that are already experts in their fields, both disbursing grants to partner organisations who support RMs and their families, as well as making grants alongside the other partners that work both within the Naval charitable sector and on a wider level (for example, SSAFA and Royal British Legion, and the Royal Naval Benevolent Trust).

With offices and representatives at NCHQ Portsmouth, Commando Training Centre Royal Marines, Scotland, London and Plymouth, the Charity is uniquely placed to understand and respond to the wide variety of challenges faced by members of the Corps Family at all stages of their lives, and to provide the support required in a swift and timely manner. Whether helping Royal Marines celebrate our unique family, dealing with life-changing injury, tackling a life-limiting illness, assisting with the transition to the civilian world, or responding to domestic crisis, it exists to support Royal Marines and their dependents should they find themselves in need wherever in the world they might be.

RMA-The Royal Marines Charity,
Building 72, Commando Training Centre Royal Marines,
Lympstone, Exmouth EX8 5AR
Tel: 02393 871564
e-mail: **enquiries@rma-trmc.org**

Royal Marines Generations

Appendix S

The Royal Marines Reserve

Formed in 1948 as the Royal Marine Forces Volunteer Reserve (RMFVR), the Royal Marines Reserve (RMR) is a force of volunteers, who undertake commando training in addition to their civilian careers. Their role is to provide commando trained manpower for operational deployments as part of RM units. The RMR also provide specialist manpower for niche tasks, including Special Forces.

Recently the RMR has undergone a period of significant change. It has been repurposed, refocussed and rejuvenated, integrating ever closer to the regular Corps and providing a RM footprint across the UK. The total strength is circa 600 all ranks. In the last ten years over 500 Reservists have mobilised in support of the Lead Commando Group and the Maritime Operations Command on ships force protection tasks and short-term training and advisory teams around the globe. They have also deployed on operations in Iraq, Afghanistan and other theatres and have been decorated for their service including two George Crosses and a US Bronze Star.

Commando training usually takes about twelve to eighteen months, which includes periods at the Commando Training Centre Royal Marines at Lympstone. RMR recruits and trained ranks routinely train during evenings and at weekends and also carry out exercises in jungle, desert, arctic and mountainous environments. RMR units and detachments are located throughout the country as follows:

RMR CITY OF LONDON   has detachments in Wandsworth, Portsmouth, Oxford and Cambridge.

RMR SCOTLAND has detachments in Edinburgh, Glasgow, Aberdeen, Dundee, Newcastle and Belfast.

RMR BRISTOL has detachments in Clifton, Cardiff, Plymouth, Poole and Lympstone.

RMR MERSEYSIDE has detachments in Liverpool, Manchester, Leeds, Birmingham and Nottingham.

Appendix T

The Royal Marines Cadets

There are three national Cadet organisations: the Sea Cadet Corps, the Combined Cadet Forces and the Volunteer Cadet Corps. All have Royal Marines Cadet detachments within them and all are open to girls and boys. In 2010, a 'Royal Favour' was granted by HM The Queen stating that every cadet wearing an RM uniform would be entitled to be called a Royal Marines Cadet, irrespective of the overarching cadet organisation to which he or she belongs. In mid 2019 there were 3,075 cadets in total. In 2011, HM The Queen graciously approved the appointment of Colonel Paul Cautley as the first Colonel Commandant Royal Marines Cadets. In 2014, to celebrate the 350th anniversary of the formation of the Corps, the different branches of the Royal Marines Cadets formally became part of the Corps Family, forming into HM Royal Marines Cadets, at a Foundation Parade on the lawns of Buckingham Palace when they received the Royal Marines Cadets Banner from the Captain General at that time, HRH The Duke of Edinburgh KG KT.

Royal Marines Detachments of the Sea Cadet Corps
The Sea Cadet Corps was established in 1899 but was not recognised by the Admiralty until twenty years later when the present title was adopted. In 1955, at the instigation of the Commandant General Royal Marines, a number of Marine Cadet Sections were formed to fit into the existing organisation of the thriving Sea Cadet Corps. There are now 141 RM Detachments in the Sea Cadet Corps and about 1,540 cadets. Besides carrying out both military and nautical training, Royal Marines Cadets learn to operate as a team, develop leadership skills and learn how to become responsible citizens. Adventurous training is a major item in Sea Cadet Corps programmes and most units operate the Duke of Edinburgh's Award scheme.

Royal Marines Detachments of the Combined Cadet Force
In the late 1850s, cadet units were established to support the Army's Volunteer Force and to provide a source of recruits for them. In 1908, the cadets were reorganised into two divisions of the Officers' Training Corps. In 1940, the junior division was retitled

the Junior Training Corps (JTC) and in 1945, when the JTC was reorganised as the Combined Cadet Force, Naval and Air Sections were incorporated. In September 1980, Royal Marines Detachments were formed within ten of the Naval Sections. There are now 24 schools across the country that have RM Detachments within the Combined Cadet Force units totalling 1,060 cadets. The cadets learn all the basic military skills such as drill, fieldcraft, administration as well as undertaking adventure training. The Detachments offer the cadets an opportunity to develop useful skills such as teamwork, leadership and the ability to work in groups whilst also gaining an insight into the Royal Marines.

Royal Marines Volunteer Cadet Corps

The first Cadet Corps in the Royal Marines was formed at Eastney in 1901. Two years later, units were also established at Chatham, Gosport, Plymouth and Deal, whilst similar naval cadet units also existed at their Port Divisions. Originally, RM Cadets were all sons of members of the Corps but in 1922 recruiting was opened to other boys. Disbanded during the Second World War, they were re-formed again in 1945. There are now 4 exclusively RM VCC units at Portsmouth, Plymouth, Lympstone and Arbroath, each one being autonomous, comprising a total of 472 cadets. Commanded by a Royal Marines officer appointed by the Commanding Officer of the parent regular unit, they use serving other ranks and civilians as instructors. Cadets are aged between nine and eighteen, dependent on the rules in each unit, and priority for entry is given to children of serving and former members of the RN and RM; although others may be considered if vacancies exist.

Appendix U

Bibliography

The following books provide recommended reading on the history of the Royal Marines and the majority should be available through any public library. They can also be consulted by making an appointment to use the reading room in the library of the National Museum of the Royal Navy in Portsmouth Historic Dockyard.

AMBLER, JOHN – *The Royal Marines Band Service* (Published by RM Historical Society 2003, Special Publication No 28)

AMBLER, JOHN & LITTLE, MATTHEW G – *Sea Soldiers of Portsmouth – Royal Marines at Eastney and Fort Cumberland* (Halsgrove, 2008)

AMBLER, JOHN – *The History of the Royal Marines Band Service* (Published by RM Historical Society, 2003. Volume II, 2011)

AMBLER, JOHN - *World War I Remembered: Royal Marine Buglers and Musicians at War* (RMHS Special Publication 2019)

ASHDOWN, LORD PADDY – *A Brilliant Little Operation: The Full Story of the Cockleshell Heroes* (Aurum Press, 2012)

BAKER, Jean - *A Marine at Gallipoli and on the Western Front: First in, Last Out - The Diary of Harry Askin* (Pen & Sword Military 2015)

BEADLE, J C – *The Light Blue Lanyard: 50 Years with 40 Commando RM* (Privately published, 1992)

BEAVER, PAUL – *Today's Royal Marines* (Patrick Stevens, 1988)

BITTNER, DONALD F - *A Soldier Gone to Sea: Memoir of a Royal Marine* in Both World Wars (McFarland & Co 2016)

BLUMBERG, IR H E – *Britain's Sea Soldiers: 1914–19* (Swift & Co. 1927 and RMHS Special Publication No 42 2014)

BROOKS, RICHARD – *The Royal Marines: 1664 to the Present* (Constable, 2002)

BROWN, JARRA - *46 Miles: A Journey of Repatriation and Humbling Respect* (Menin House 2015)

BRUCE LOCKHART, SIR ROBERT – *The Marines Were There* (Putnam, 1950)

CLAPP, MICHAEL & SOUTHBY-TAILYOUR, EWEN – *Amphibious Assault Falklands: The Battle of San Carlos Water* (Orion, 1996)

CROCKETT, ANTHONY – *Green Beret, Red Star* (Eyre & Spottiswood, 1954)

CROUCHER, MATT GC – *Bullet Proof* (Century, 2009)

DE BOLSTER, MARC - *47 Royal Marine Commando: An Inside Story 1943-1946* (Fonthill Media 2014)

EDWARDS, BRIAN - *Formative Years 1803 to 1806: a Perspective of the Royal Marines in the Navy of John Jervis, Earl St Vincent and Horatio, Lord Nelson* (RMHS Special Publication No 31 2005)

EDWARDS, BRIAN (EDITOR)– *After Limbang, A Royal Marines Anthology of Experiences of the Confrontation with Indonesia December 1962 to September 1966* (RMHS Special Publication No 36)

EDYE, L – *Historical Records of The Royal Marines: Vol I* (Harrison, 1893)

FIELD, COLONEL CYRIL – *Britain's Sea Soldiers* (Lyceum Press, 1924)

FORD, KEN – *D-Day Commando: From Normandy to the Maas with 48 RM Commando* (Sutton Publishing, 2003)

FORD, KEN – *The Cockleshell Raid, Bordeaux 1942* (Osprey, 2010)

FORFAR, JOHN – *From Omaha to the Scheldt: The Story of 47 RM Commando* (Tuckwell Press, 2001)

FOSTER, NIGEL – *Making of a Royal Marine Commando* (Sidgwick & Jackson, 1987)

FRASER, E AND CARR-LAUGHTON, L G – *The Royal Marine Artillery* (RUSI, 1930)

GARDINER, IAN – *The Yompers: With 45 Commando in the Falklands War* (Pen and Sword, 2012)

GROVER, G – *Short History of the Royal Marines* (Gale & Polden, Second Edition, 1959)

HAMPSHIRE, A CECIL – *The Royal Marines Tercentenary* (The Commandant General Royal Marines, 1964)

HAYHURST, FRED – *Green Berets In Korea* (Vanguard Press, 2003)

HMSO – *The Royal Marines: The Admiralty record of their achievements 1939–1943*

HOLLIS, SIR LESLIE – *One Marine's Tale* (Andre Deutsch 1956)

HOLLOWAY, SM - *From trench and turret: Royal Marines letters and diaries 1914-1918* (Royal Marines Museum; 1990)

JENKINS, W G – *Commando Subaltern at War: RM Operations in Yugoslavia and Italy 1944/45* (Greenhill, 1996)

Appendices

LADD, JAMES D – *By Sea By Land: The Authorised History of the Royal Marines Commandos* (Harper Collins, 1999)

LADD, JAMES D – *Royal Marine Commando* (Hamlyn, 1982)

LADD, JAMES D – *Commandos and Rangers of The Second World War* (Macdonald and Jane's, 1978)

LADD, JAMES D – *Inside the Commandos* (Arms and Armour Press, 1984)

LADD, JAMES D – *SBS – The Invisible Raiders* (Arms and Armour Press, 1983)

LANE, ANDREW – *The Royal Marines Barracks Eastney: A Pictorial History* (Halsgrove, 1998)

LANE, ANDREW – *Royal Marines Deal: A Pictorial History* (Halsgrove, 2000)

LANE, ANDREW – *Royal Marines Commandos in the Falklands War: A Pictorial History* (Halsgrove, 2000)

LITTLE, MATTHEW G – T*he Royal Marines & the Victoria Cross* (RM Museum, 2002)

LITTLE, MATTHEW G & BROOKS, RICHARD – *Tracing your Royal Marines Ancestors* (Pen and Sword, 2008)

LOCKHART, SIR ROBERT BRUCE KCMG – *The Marines Were There: The Story of the Royal Marines in the Second World War* (Putnam, 1950)

LOVERING, T T A (EDITOR) – *Amphibious Assault: Manoeuvre from the Sea* (Seafarer Books, 2007)

LYMAN, ROBERT – *Operation Suicide – The Remarkable Story of the Cockleshell Raid* (Quercus, 2012)

MARSH, A E – *Flying Marines* (Privately published, 1980)

MCCONVILLE, MICHAEL – *Nothing Much To Lose: The Story of 2nd Battalion Royal Marines and 43 Commando Royal Marines* (Privately published, 1992)

MCCONVILLE, MICHAEL – *Tell it to the Royal Marines: A Royal Marines Ragbag* (Cross Publishing, 2003)

MACKENZIE, TONY – *44(RM) Commando – Achnacarry to the Arakan: A Diary of the Commando at War, August 1943 to March 1947* (Tom Donovan, 1996)

MILES, ALBERT – *The Shadow on my Evening* (Vanguard Press, 2001)

MITCHELL, RAYMOND – *They Did What Was Asked of Them: 41 (Royal Marines) Commando 1942–1946* (Firebird Books, 1996)

MITCHELL, RAYMOND – *Marine Commando: Sicily and Salerno with 41 RM Commando* (Robert Hale, 1988)

179

MOULTON, J L – *The Royal Marines* (RM Museum, 1981)

MOULTON, J L – *Haste to the Battle: A Marine Commando at War* (Cassell, 1963)

MOULTON, JL – *Battle for Antwerp* (Ian Allan 1978)

NEILLANDS, ROBIN – *By Sea and Land* (Weidenfeld & Nicholson, 1987)

NICOLAS, PAUL H – *Historical Record of the Royal Marine Forces* (Boone, 1845)

NICOLAS, PAUL H, - *The History of the Royal Marines: the Early Years 1664-1842: Volume 1* (Leonaur 2014)

NICHOLAS, PAUL H, - *The History of the Royal Marines: the Early Years 1664-1842: Volume 2,* (Leonaur 2014)

NORMAN, MIKE & JONES, MICHAEL - T*he Falklands War - There and Back Again: The Story of Naval Party 8901* (Pen & Sword Military 2019)

NUTTING, DAVID (EDITOR) – *Attain by Surprise: The Story of 30 Assault Unit – Intelligence by Capture in WW II* (David Colver, 1997)

OAKLEY, DEREK & SMITH, PETER C – *The Royal Marines* (Spellmount, 1988)

OAKLEY, DEREK – *The Royal Marines into the Nineties* (Commandant General Royal Marines, 1993)

OAKLEY, DEREK – *Fiddler On The March: A Biography of Lieutenant Colonel Sir Vivian Dunn* (RM Historical Society, 2000)

OAKLEY, DEREK – *The Commandos: World War Two to the Present* (Arms and Armour Press, 1987)

PARKER, JOHN – *SBS - The Inside Story of the Special Boat Service*

PHILLIPS, C E LUCAS – *Cockleshell Heroes* (Heinemann, 1956)

QUICK, STANLEY L, REID, CHIP - *Lion in the Bay: The British Invasion of the Chesapeake, 1813-14* (Naval Institute Press 2015)

RAWLINSON, JOHN – *Personal Distinctions, 350 Years of Royal Marines Uniforms and Insignia* (RMHS Special Publication 41, 2014)

REECE, M J – *Flying Royal Marines* (RMHS, 2012)

REYNOLDS, DAVID – *Commando: The Illustrated History of Britain's Green Berets from Dieppe to Afghanistan* (Sutton, 2001)

ROSE, MARKHAM – *The Story of the Royal Marines* (Seventh Edition, 1935)

SMITH, PETER C – *Per Mare Per Terram* (Balfour, 1974)

SOUTHBY-TAILYOUR, EWEN – *Reasons in Writing: A Commando's View of the Falklands War* (Leo Cooper, 1993)

Appendices

SOUTHBY-TAILYOUR, EWEN - *Blondie: Founder of the SBS and Modern Single Handed Ocean Racing* (Leo Cooper 1998)

SOUTHBY-TAILYOUR, EWEN - *Helmand, Afghanistan, 3 Commando Brigade* (Ebury Publishing, 2008)

SOUTHBY-TAILYOUR, EWEN - 3 *Commando Brigade Helmand Assault* (Ebury Publishing, 2010)

STADDEN, NEWARK AND DONALD - *Uniforms of the Royal Marines from 1664 to the present day* (Pompadour Gallery, 1997)

STEVENS, PADDY - *The Long Summer, 45 Commando RM 1963-64, Aden, Tanganyika and the Radfan* (RMHS - Special Publication No 35, 2009)

TAYLOR, KEITH - *The waist-high cornfield: the story of the 46 Royal Marine Commando and the battle for Rots in Normandy* (Privately published 2017)

THOMAS, GARETH - *Records Of The Royal Marines: PRO Readers'Guide No 10* (PRO Publications, 1994)

THOMPSON, JULIAN - T*he Royal Marines: From Sea Soldiers to a Special Force* (Sidgwick & Jackson, 2000)

THOMPSON, JULIAN - *No Picnic – 3 Commando Brigade in the South Atlantic: 1982* (Leo ooper/Secker and Warburg 1985)

TOWNSEND, FREDDIE OBE - *A Most Unlikely Marine* (Privately Published 2004)

TRENDELL, JOHN - *Colonel Bogey to the Fore* (The Blue Band Magazine, 1991)

VAUX, NICK - *March to the South Atlantic* (Buchan and Enright, 1986)

YOUNG, DAVID - *Four Five – The Story of 45 Commando RM 1943–1971* (Leo Cooper, 1972)

YOUNG, JOHN ROBERT - *The Royal Marines* (Guild Publishing, 1991)

ZERBE, BRITT - *The Birth of the Royal Marines, 1664-1802,* (Boydell Press, 2013)

Nothing Impossible: *A Portrait of the Royal Marines* (Third Millennium Publishing, 2010)

The Royal Marines (Pitkin Pictorials Ltd, 1971)

The Royal Marines Museum – The Story of Britain's Sea Soldiers (RM Museum, 1989)

1664–1964 – An Account of the Royal Marines Tercentenary Celebrations (Privately published, 1964)

Royal Marines Prayers

The Royal Marines Prayer

O Eternal Lord God, who through many generations has united and inspired the members of our Corps, grant Thy blessing, we beseech Thee, on Royal Marines serving all round the GLOBE. Bestow Thy CROWN of Righteousness upon all our efforts and endeavours and may our LAURELS be those of gallantry and honour, loyalty and courage. We ask these things in the Name of Him, whose courage never failed, our Redeemer, Jesus Christ. AMEN

A memorial service in Afghanistan 2002 to commemorate the twentieth anniversary of the Falklands Campaign.

The Royal Marines Band Service Prayer

Almighty and eternal Lord God, in whose sight and love live our memories of many generations of those who have served You in the Band Service of the Royal Marines: we thank You for the rich heritage of music placed in our hands, and for the joy and inspiration which it brings to men; enable us with our whole hearts to serve You, that by Your grace and through our gift of music, we may continue to inspire, help and lead men; we ask these things in the name of Jesus Christ our Lord. AMEN

Appendices

The Commando Prayer

Teach us, Good Lord, to Serve Thee as Thou deservest;
To give and not to count the cost; to fight and not to heed the wounds;
To toil and not seek for rest; to labour and not to ask any reward,
Save that of knowing that we do Thy Holy Will.
Through Jesus Christ Our Lord, Amen.

At Royal Marines church and drum-head services the following special fourth verse of Eternal Father strong to save is often sung:

O, Holy Spirit grant, we pray
To Royal Marines, both night and day,
The courage, honour, strength and skill
Their land to serve, Thy law fulfil
Be Thou our shield forever more
From every peril to our Corps.

Under the watchful eye of a Marine armed with a GPMG, the Chaplain of 45 Commando, using a makeshift altar, conducts a service during operations in the Radfan, 1963.

A Brief Chronology of Principal Events

1664: Formation of the Duke of York and Albany's Maritime Regt of Foot.
1665–72: 2nd & 3rd Dutch Wars. Royal Netherlands Marine Corps formed.
1685: Renamed Prince George of Denmark's Regt – disbanded 1689.
1689–97: War with France.
1702–13: War of Spanish Succession. Six Regts of Marines formed.
1704: British and Dutch Marines capture Gibraltar.
1713: Reduced to three Regts which were transferred to the Line. Only four Companies of Marine Invalids remained.
1739: England declared war on Spain – The War of Jenkins' Ear. Six Marine Regiments raised.
1740: Further four Regts raised.
1745–1750: Hannah Snell served in the Marines.
1748: The Peace of Aix-la-Chapelle. All ten Marine Regts disbanded.
1755: A permanent Marine Corps of 50 Independent Companies established.
Corps Strength 5,000.
1756: The Seven Years War.
Corps Strength 19,000.
1759: The Capture of Quebec.

1761: The Capture of Belleisle.
1770: Marines land with Captain James Cook at Botany Bay, Australia.
1775: American War of Independence. The Battle of Bunker Hill. US Marine Corps formed.
1776: Corps Strength 25,000.
1783: Stonehouse Barracks first occupied.
1788: Marines from the First Fleet land in Australia.
1793–1802: French Revolutionary Wars – Actions in the Mediterranean, South Africa, India, Egypt and the East Indies.
1794: The Battle of the Glorious First of June off Ushant.
1797: The Battles of Camperdown and Cape St Vincent.
1798: The Battle of the Nile.
1802: The Corps honoured with the title 'Royal'.
1803–15: Napoleonic Wars – Actions in East and West Indies, South America, South Africa and others.
1804: RM Artillery Companies formed.
1805: The Battle of Trafalgar. Woolwich Div formed.
Corps Strength 31,000.

Appendices

1812–15: The War of 1812 in America.
1814: The sacking of Washington.
1815: Napoleon exiled to St Helena.
1816: The bombardment of Algiers.
1820: King George IV directed RM would take precedence after 49th Regt.
1827: Colours presented to each of the Divs by HRH The Duke of Clarence. 'The Globe' badge granted.
Corps Strength 9,000.
1835–0: RM Bn and RMA Bty in Spain during the Carlist War.
1839: RM from HM ships *Volage* and *Cruiser* served with combined force that captured Aden.
1839–42: RM in action in China's Opium wars.
1848: Portsmouth Div moved into Forton Barracks, Gosport.
1854–56: The Crimean War.
1854: Battle of Inkerman – first Royal Marine awarded Victoria Cross – Corporal Prettyjohns.
1855: Royal Marines designated Light Infantry.
Corps Strength 15,500.
1856–60: 2nd China War.
1857–58: Indian Mutiny.
1861: Depot established at Deal.
1861–64: The Maori Wars in New Zealand.
1861–62: RM Bn in Mexico.
1862: RMA & RMLI became separate Corps.
1864 Eastney Barracks first occupied.
1864–65: RM Bn in Japan.
1867–68: Expedition to Abyssinia.
1868: RM Bn in Ireland.
1869: Woolwich Div closed.
1870: RM Bn in Japan.
1873–74: The Ashanti War.
1879: The Zulu War.
1880–83: RM Bn in Ireland.
1882: The Egyptian Campaign.
1884–85: The Sudan Campaign.
1899–1902: RM with the Naval Brigade in South Africa.
Corps Strength 19,000.
1900–01: RM in action during the Boxer Rebellion alongside the USMC (for the first time).
1903: Royal Naval School of Music formed at Eastney. RM Memorial in the Mall unveiled.
1914–18: First World War. Marines in HM Ships in all major engagements at sea.
1914: RM Bde at Ostend and Antwerp.
1914: (Aug) Corps Strength 18,234.
1915: RM Bde with the RN Div in Gallipoli. RMA Howitzer and AA. Bdes & Heavy Siege Train to France and Flanders.
1916: RM Bns to France with 63rd (RN) Div. Battle of Jutland.

1918: The Raid on Zeebrugge – 4th RM Bn. Institution of King's Squad & King's Badge.
Corps Strength 55,000.
1919: 6th Bn in North Russia.
1922: 8th Bn in Ireland.
1923: 11th Bn in Turkey. Amalgamation of RMA and RMLI. Forton Barracks, Gosport closed.
1927: 12th Bn in Shanghai.
1930: RN School of Music moved to Deal.
1935: RM carryout London Duties London for the first time. RM in Alexandria with Base Defences, Mediterranean.
Corps Strength 9,800.
1939–45: Second World War. Marines in HM Ships in all major engagements at sea.
1940: RM ashore in Faroe Islands, Iceland, Norway, Holland and France.
1941: MNBDO1 in the evacuation of Crete. HMS *Prince of Wales* and *Repulse* sunk.
1942: 'Plymouth Argylls' in Singapore. Force VIPER in Burma. First RM Commando formed. 40 RM Cdo at Dieppe. 11th RM Bn at Tobruk. Op Frankton – Cockleshell Heroes raid on Bordeaux shipping.
1943: 40 & 41 Cdos land in Sicily. 41 Cdo landed at Salerno. RM Bns formed into Cdos. 40 & 43 Cdos in action in Italy, Albania and Yugoslavia.
1944: 43 Cdo landed at Anzio. 48 Cdo formed. 17,500 Marines in The Landings in Normandy, serving in Cdos, HM Ships and Landing Craft. 41, 47 & 48 Cdos in the Assault on Walcheren, supported by Marines in HM Ships and landing craft.
1945: 42 & 44 Cdos in the Battle of Kangaw, Burma. 40 & 43 Cdos in the Battle of Lake Comacchio, Italy. RM Cdos in the river crossings in NW Europe.
Corps Strength 78,500.
1946: Marines from HM Ships occupy Penang. 42 & 44 Cdos occupy Hong Kong.
1947: Reorganisation of the Corps – RM Divs become functional Gps.
1948: RM Cdos cover the withdrawal from Palestine and deployed in the Suez Canal Zone. RM Forces Volunteer Reserve formed.
1949: 45 Cdo in Egyt and Aqaba. 3 Cdo Bde moves to Hong Kong. Closure of Chatham Gp.
1950: 3 Cdo Bde moved to Malaya. 41 Independent Cdo formed for operations in Korea. Chatham Barracks closed. RM Div Bands integrated with the RN School of Music to form the Royal Marines School of Music.
1952: 3 Cdo Bde moved to Malta. Presentation of first Colours to the

Appendices

RM Cdos.

41 Independent Cdo disbanded at Bickleigh.

1953: 3 Cdo Bde moved to the Suez Canal Zone. HRH The Duke of Edinburgh appointed Captain General Royal Marines.

1954: 40 & 45 Cdos returned to Malta.

42 Cdo moves to UK Amphibious School RM moved to Poole.

1955–59: 40 & 45 Cdos alternated on operations in Cyprus.

1956: 3 Cdo Bde spearheaded landings at Port Said. First RM detachments for frigates formed. Corps Strength 10,000.

1957: Elements of 42 Cdo in Northern Ireland. Small Arms School RM at Browndown closed.

1958: RM Gunnery School at Eastney closed.

1960: HMS *Bulwark* commissioned as first Cdo Ship. 45 Cdo moved to Aden.

42 Cdo moved to Singapore. 41 Cdo re-formed. Melville Barracks Chatham closed. Green Berets to be worn by all trained ranks.

1961: 42 & 45 Cdos landed in Kuwait. HQ 3 Cdo Bde established in Singapore.

43 Cdo re-formed in Plymouth.

1962: 40 & 42 Cdos in Brunei.

Limbang Operation.

1963–66: 3 Cdo Bde (less 45 Cdo) in anti-terrorist Confrontation operations in Borneo and Malaysia.

1964: 41 & 45 Cdos in East Africa. Corps Tercentenary celebrations. Lovat Dress introduced.

1964–1967: 45 Cdo on operations in the Radfan.

1965: Earl Mountbatten of Burma appointed a Colonel Commandant RM.

1966: The RMFVR retitled Royal Marines Reserve. End of Indonesian Confrontation.

1967: 42 Cdo covered the final withdrawal from Aden (The Corps was also present at the capture of the port in 1839). 45 Cdo returned to UK. 40 Cdo on IS duties in Hong Kong.

1968: 43 Cdo disbanded.

1969: 41 Cdo was the first RM Cdo on operations in Northern Ireland.

1970: Title of Infantry Training Centre RM changed to Commando Training Centre RM. 45 Cdo assigned to NATO for the Northern Flank.

1971: 3 Cdo Bde returned to UK from the Far East. 41 Cdo moved to Malta. 45 Cdo moved to Arbroath.

1972: Cdo Logistic Regiment formed. Warrant rank reintroduced.

1973: PRORM integrated with

HMS *Centurion*.
1974: 40 & 41 Cdos with UN Forces in Cyprus.
Corps Strength 7,000.
1976: RM detachments in frigates during the Cod War off Iceland.
1977: Silver Jubilee Inspection by HM The Queen on Plymouth Hoe. 41 Cdo (less Salerno Company) left Malta.
1978: First 10-man Frigate detachment formed. 41 Cdo carried out London Duties.
1979: Salerno Company left Malta.. 42 Cdo deployed to Hong Kong for IS duties. Earl Mountbatten assassinated by the IRA.
1980: Comacchio Company formed (later Fleet Protection Gp RM). Elements of 42 Cdo deployed to the New Hebrides (Vanuatu). 3rd Raiding Sqn deployed to Hong Kong for duties against illegal immigrants.
1981: HRH Crown Prince Harald (now HM The King of Norway) appointed Hon Colonel Royal Marines. 41 Cdo disbanded at Deal. The Commandant General, Lieutenant General Sir Steuart Pringle blown up outside his house by a terrorist car bomb.
1982: 3 Cdo Bde spearheaded the recapture of the Falkland Islands. RM Detachment for NP 1002 first

deployed to Diego Garcia. 3 Cdo Bde Air Sqn moved to RNAS Yeovilton.
Corps Strength 7,900 (10.8% of RN).
1983: 40 Cdo deployed to Cyprus for UN tour of duty. RM Band of Flag Officer Naval Air Command disbanded.
40 Cdo moved to Taunton.
1984: Detachments of 3 Cdo Bde Air Defence Troop embarked in ships of the Armilla Patrol. HM The Queen visited RM Poole. 539 Assault Sqn formed. All 10-man Frigate detachments withdrawn.
1985–93: RM Cdos deployed on operational tours in Belize.
1986: 42 Cdo carried out London Duties. RM Cdo memorial unveiled at Lympstone.
1987: RM Band of Flag Officer 3rd Flotilla (FOF3) disbanded. SBS titled Special Boat Service and came under command of Director Special Forces.
1988: 3 RSRM disbanded in Hong Kong. Hong Kong Sqn Dets formed.
1989: IRA bomb exploded at RMSM Deal killing 11 band ranks.
1990: RM embarked in HM Ships during the Gulf War.
1991: HQ Cdo Forces and 3 Cdo Bde (less 42 Cdo) deployed to South East Turkey for Operation HAVEN. Eastney Barracks closed.
Corps strength 7400, (11.9% of RN).

Appendices

1992: Alliance with the Barbados Defence Force.

1994: 45 Cdo deployed to Kuwait.

1995: Headquarters Royal Marines established on Whale Island, Portsmouth. 3 Cdo Bde Air Sqn incorporated into Naval Air Command as 847 Naval Air Sqn. RM provided the Commander and the Operations Staff of the Rapid Reaction Force HQ in Bosnia. Cdo Log Regt moved to Chivenor. 42 Cdo and elements of the Cdo Logistic Regt on humanitarian and disaster relief in the West Indies. DRORM closed.

1996: Royal Marines School of Music moved to Portsmouth.

1996–97: 42 Cdo and a detachment from 539 ASRM in the Congo prepared to evacuate civilians from Kinshasa.

1998: 45 Cdo on humanitarian and disaster relief in Honduras and Nicaragua. 40 Cdo and a detachment from 539 ASRM in the Congo prepared to evacuate British Nationals.

1999: Ranks of RM Officers aligned to those of the Army.

2000: 42 Cdo deployed to Sierra Leone. HQ 3 Cdo Brigade, 45 Cdo, the Cdo Log Regt and the RM Band Plymouth deployed to Kosovo.

RM National Memorial in London rededicated. Comacchio Gp renamed Fleet Protection Gp RM.

2001: Fleet Protection Gp moved from Arbroath to Faslane. New Colours presented to 40, 42 and 45 Cdos at Plymouth. Elements of 40 Cdo deployed in HMS Ocean for operations in Afghanistan. 3 Cdo Bde Sigs Sqn RM renamed United Kingdom Landing Force Command Support Gp. RM Poole renamed 1 Assault Gp.

2002: 45 Cdo Gp deployed on operations in Afghanistan. Headquarters United Kingdom Amphibious Force established with the Commandant General as COMUKAMPHIBFOR. Firefighters' Industrial action, over 600 RM (incl 150 Band) ranks involved. 42 Cdo N Ireland tour. (Apr) <u>Corps Strength 7,010 (16.8% of RN).</u>

2003: The Iraq War. Op TELIC – 3 Cdo Bde operations on the Al Faw peninsula. Viking armoured vehicle introduced, Armoured Sp Coy established.

2004: 40 Cdo Operational tour in Iraq.

45 Cdo completed final operational deployment to Northern Ireland. Bowman Communications System

introduced. Viking entered service with 3 Cdo Bde.

2005: C O M U K A M P H I B F O R deployed to Iraq with his HQ to command Multi-National Division, Southeast. 'Trafalgar 200' ceremonies.

2006: 3 Cdo Bde in Norway for Winter Deployment, then to Helmand, Afghanistan (less 40 Cdo). Op HERRICK 5. Staff of COMUKAMPHIBFOR provide augmentees to ISAF and Bde HQ. CGRM Dep Comd Stability in ISAF and Senior Brit Milrep to Dec 07.

2007: 3 Cdo Bde return to UK. Armoured Sp Coy RM (Afghanistan) remained in theatre to support Army units. Armed Sp Gp RM formed at Bovington. 40 Cdo to Afghanistan Op HERRICK 7. SBS assumes ownership of Royal Marines Poole.

2008: 1 Rifles join 3 Cdo Bde. 24 Cdo Engr Regt formed. 3 Cdo Bde (-40 Cdo) to Afghanistan Op HERRICK 9. HQ & Sp Sqn of 1 Asslt Gp move from Poole to Devonport, 10 LC Trg Sqn remains at Poole.

2009: Hasler Coy opened in HMS *Drake*. RM Memorial Wall unveiled at CTCRM.

2010: 40 Cdo Op HERRICK 12. Op ATALANTA COMUKAMPHIBFOR command EU mission to combat piracy off coast of Somalia. UKLF CSG renamed as 3 Cdo IX Gp RM.

2011: 3 Cdo Bde (-40 Cdo) Op HERRICK 14.

2012: FPGRM renamed as 43 Cdo FP Gp RM and becomes part of 3 Cdo Bde RM. RMR Tyne subordinated under RMR Scotland. Corps Strength 7890 (22.2% of RN – Apr 2012).

2013: 1Rifles leaves 3 Cdo Bde. HQ 1 AGRM. RM Tamar opened. Operation PATWIN – J Coy 42 Cdo RM Humanitarian Assistance operations in the Philippines. 30 Cdo IX Gp RM freedom of Littlehampton

2014: RM 350. Foundation parade of HM Rm Cadets. Operation PITCHPOLE 40 Cdo RM. 42 Cdo RM London Duties. Operation GRITROCK – 42 Cdo and 1 AGRM humanitarian Assistance to Ebola crisis in Sierra Leone.

<u>Corps Strength 6680, (28% of RN)</u>

2015: Operation WEALD – Elements 45 Cdo RM embarked on HMS *Bulwark* rescuing migrants in the Mediterranean. 45 Cdo RM Freedom of East Lincolnshire.

2016: Operations SILVAN and LITTEN– RM detachments on Border Force ships in response to refugee crisis in Mediterranean. Announcement by Prime Minister lifting restrictions on women serving in the GCC role to be lifted from 1 Jan 2019.

2017: HRH The Prince Harry of Wales announced as Captain General in succession to HRH The Duke of Edinburgh. RM Museum Eastney closes public galleries. RMR City of London Freedom of Wandsworth. Operation Ruman, 40 Cdo Gp disaster relief in West Indies.

Corps Strength 6570, (27.6% of RN)

2018: Project Sykes, reorganization of 3 Cdo Bde RM and 42 Cdo RM becomes the Maritime Operations Commando. Royal Marines Freedom of the City of Birmingham. HMS *Queen Elizabeth* enters service. First deployments of Special Purpose Task Groups.

2019: 40 Cdo RM awarded a fourth Sword of Peace.

Appendix X

Corps Etiquette

General

Whilst the precise application of the following customs may vary according to context and local orders, the following guidance should generally be used by all serving members of the Corps. More detail can be found in BRd 1283 – Royal Marines Instructions and in BRd 2118 - Royal Marines Drill. In cases of doubt, guidance should be sought from the RM Corps Secretariat.

Standing Up for the Regimental Marches

Whenever the Royal Marines Regimental March, 'A Life on the Ocean Wave' is played, Royal Marines not in formed bodies should stand to attention as a mark of their pride in the Corps. This custom applies to both those in uniform and those in civilian clothes. Those in formed bodies are to comply with relevant parade orders. This custom also applies to those attending formal dinners and musical concerts. Veteran Royal Marines are encouraged to follow this custom.

Saluting

THE NATIONAL ANTHEM. Personnel in uniform not paraded as part of a formed sub-unit should stand to attention and salute whenever the National Anthem is played. The same courtesy should also be extended when other countries' national anthems are played.

THE LAST POST AND REVEILLE. Whenever the Last Post and Reveille are sounded as an act of homage, ie at Remembrance Day services and funerals, personnel in uniform not paraded as part of a formed sub-unit should stand to attention and salute on the first note of the Last Post bugle call. At the last note personnel cease saluting and remain at attention during the two minutes silence. When RMA Standards are on parade they will similarly be lowered on the first note of the Last Post but are not returned to the Carry until the first note of Reveille.

Appendices

COLOURS AND SUNSET. If attending a ceremonial Sunset, eg. as part of a Ceremony of Beating Retreat, personnel in uniform not paraded, as part of a formed sub-unit, should stand to attention and salute when the tune Sunset is played as the White Ensign is lowered. Personnel on the upper decks of a Royal Navy ship or outdoors in a Naval Shore Establishment should stand to attention and salute when the 'Still' is piped during morning Colours or evening Sunset whenever the White Ensign is being raised or lowered. When the 'Carry On' is piped, personnel should come down from the salute and carry on with their business. Serving personnel in civilian clothes should stand to attention but not salute. The important point to note is that it is the raising and lowering of the White Ensign that is being respected, not the playing of 'Sunset'.

GOING ONBOARD HM SHIPS AND PROCEEDING ASHORE. Personnel in uniform should pause at the top of the brow and salute whenever going onboard or proceeding ashore from a commissioned ship of the Royal Navy. The same courtesy should be extended to foreign warships, RFAs and merchant ships.

SALUTING IN SMALL GROUPS. Serving personnel in uniform moving around barracks or elsewhere in informal groups should all salute if they pass a commissioned Officer senior to the most senior person in their group. If that senior Officer is himself accompanied by others, only the senior Officer present should return the salute.

WHEN ROYALTY, A VIP OR A SENIOR OFFICER RECEIVES A SALUTE ON PARADE. Whenever a member of the Royal Family, a VIP or a Senior Officer is given a Royal Salute or a General Salute on parade, only the person being saluted returns the salute. Uniformed individuals attending the person being saluted remain at attention and do not salute. Similarly, uniformed spectators in stands behind the VIP do not salute, unless the salute being played is the National Anthem.

Addressing personnel of different rank

Serving personnel should normally formally address those senior in rank to themselves on at least the first occasion of meeting each day and on any other occasion when formality is appropriate eg if called to an office or if being reprimanded. More junior personnel should be particularly diligent in observing this custom, as should those who do not know each other well. More senior personnel should make it clear when informality is acceptable (eg when playing sport) and when it is not. Styles of address are:

Rank	By those Junior	By those Senior	Referring to third parties in conversation
(a)	(b)	(c)	(d)
LCorporals and Corporals	Corporal	Corporal	Corporal Name
Sgts	Sergeant	Sergeant	Sergeant Name
CSgts	Colour Sergeant	Colour Sergeant	Colour Sergeant Name
WO2s	Sergeant Major	Sergeant Major	Mister Name
WO1s	Sir	Mister Name	Mister Name
WO1 (RSMs)	Sir	RSM	Mister Name
2Lts and Lts	Sir	Mister Name	Mister Name
Capts	Sir	Captain Name	Captain Name
Majs	Sir	Major Name	Major Name
Lieutenant Cols and Cols	Sir (or Colonel)	Colonel Name	Colonel Name
Brigs	Sir (or Brigadier)	Brigadier Name	Brigadier Name
General Officers	Sir (or General)	General Name	General Name

The Colours

Colours have been carried in the Corps since the first Marine regiment was raised in 1664. At that time each company carried its own colour, which were all based on the yellow of the uniform. For succeeding regiments the company Colours were altered with the times and to suit changes in the uniform.

By the time the Corps was reformed in 1755 as fifty independent companies, the number of Colours in an Army battalion had been reduced to two. Colours do not appear to have been issued at first, probably because the independent companies were distributed between Chatham, Portsmouth and Plymouth and not organised as battalions. However, in 1760, when a battalion was formed for the expedition to Belleisle, Colours were provided. In the Army the King's or First Colour was based on the Union Flag and the Second Colour on a flag to match the regimental facings; the coloured material of the turned back skirts, lapels, collar and cuffs of the long coat worn at that time. However, the Marines appear not to have followed this custom completely in that the principal colour of the Second Colour seems to have been crimson. Soon after this, a stand of Colours was presented to each of the three Divisions. The central devices were the same on both Colours, namely a foul anchor within a wreath of roses and thistles.

It had long been the custom for 'Royal' regiments to have blue facings and so, after the Corps was so honoured in 1802 and when new Colours were presented in 1811, the Second Colour, which by then was unofficially known as the Regimental Colour, was blue and so it has remained to the present day.

The first Colours with devices similar to those borne today date back to 1827, when HRH The Duke of Clarence, later King William IV, the 'Sailor King', presented a stand to each Division. By this time in the Army it had become customary to embroider on the Colours battle honours which had been awarded to the regiment. In one of his speeches HRH spoke of this when commenting on the devices borne and said:

> "The greatness of the number of actions to be considered and the difficulty of selecting amidst so many glorious deeds such a portion as could be inserted in this space, determined His Majesty King George IV to direct that The Globe encircled with Laurel should be the distinguishing badge as the most

appropriate emblem of a Corps whose duties carry them to all parts of the Globe, in every quarter of which they had earned laurels by their valour and good conduct…"

He pointed out that the honour **GIBRALTAR** was for the Capture and Defence in 1704–5 and he knew that *"…Marines were engaged in this capture and none but Marines were employed by the Prince of Hesse in the glorious defence…"*, and further directed that from the difficulty of selecting battle honours amidst so many glorious deeds, the Corps should have the 'Great Globe itself' as its emblem to be surrounded by the Laurel Wreath, retaining Gibraltar as the first great battle honour to represent all previous and subsequent honours.

His Royal Highness went on to say that:

*"…His Majesty has given them the most peculiar and honourable distinction, a badge of his own Cypher; and further, His Majesty directed that whatever King and Queen they might serve under hereafter, though the Cypher of the reigning Sovereign must appear on their Standard, still in those of the Royal Marines, the **Cypher GRIV** was forever to appear."*

He also said that the cypher was being added to that peculiar badge (The Anchor), *"…which is your distinctive bearing"* and drew attention to *"… the motto, peculiarly your own, 'PER MARE PER TERRAM' has been allowed to remain…"*

In 1858 new Colours were presented to each of the four Divisions by the local Naval Cs-in-C with very little ceremony. The design followed a new pattern for Colours in the Army and departed from the embellishments authorised by King George IV. This change was most unpopular in the Corps and it is not surprising that when new stands were to be presented in 1894 and 1896, the 1827 design returned. However that was not the only change that was made. Until the middle of the nineteenth century Colours were nearly six foot square, on a 9ft 10in pike and were carried by very young officers, often mere boys in their late teens. These young men had considerable difficulty in controlling the Colours when they were unfurled, when even a slight breeze could carry them off their feet and they sometimes suffered the indignity of being thrown to the ground. The 1894 and 1896 stands were the first of a new smaller pattern to be carried in the Corps, 3ft 9in by 3ft, and the same size as those borne today.

In 1947, on the reorganisation into RM Groups, the Colours of Chatham, Portsmouth and Plymouth Divisions automatically became the Colours of RM

Appendices

Barracks, Chatham, Eastney and Plymouth respectively. The last of these to be carried were those of RM Barracks, Eastney presented in 1956 and which were finally laid up in the Corps Museum in 1973. Since then only 40, 41, 42 and 45 Commandos have carried Colours in the Royal Marines since only they retain the roles and traditions of infantry units; specialist RM units are thus not entitled to carry Colours.

Colours were first presented to Commandos in 1952, when HRH The Duke of Edinburgh presented a stand to each of the three units of 3 Commando Brigade RM in Malta. The Colours presented to 40 Commando RM at that time were laid up in the Corps Museum when new Colours were presented in 1976. Those of 42 Commando RM are now in the Officers' Mess at the Commando Training Centre RM, Lympstone, the unit having received a new stand in Singapore in 1968. In the following year HM The Queen presented new Colours to 45 Commando RM in Plymouth, and their original stand was laid up in Stationers Hall in the City of London.

41 and 43 Commandos were reformed in 1960 and 1961 respectively and also received Colours. When 41 Commando disbanded their Colours were laid up in the Officers' Mess at Stonehouse Barracks, Plymouth but are now in the RM Museum at the NMRN, whilst 43 Commando's Colours are kept by 43 Commando Fleet Protection Group Royal Marines.

New stands of Colours were presented to 40, 42 and 45 Commandos by the Captain General at a parade held on Plymouth Hoe on 12 July 2001.

The previous Colours of 40 Commando RM are laid up in St Lawrence Jewry next Guildhall in the City of London, the Corps' affiliated church (see Appendix G), those of 42 Commando are in the Falklands Hall at the Commando Training Centre RM, and 45 Commando's previous Colours are in the Officers' Mess at Stonehouse Barracks.

In the Royal Marines there have only been two occasions when the Sovereign has presented Colours. Queen Victoria presented Colours to Portsmouth Division RMLI at Osborne House on the Isle of Wight in 1894. Her Majesty Queen Elizabeth II presented Colours to 45 Commando RM in Plymouth in 1969, but all the remainder since 1951 have been presented by HRH The Prince Philip, Duke of Edinburgh, including the last Colours to be borne by RM Barracks, Plymouth and RM Barracks, Eastney. The presentations to RM Barracks, Plymouth and the three units of 3 Commando Brigade in Malta were even prior to the appointment of HRH as Captain General Royal Marines.

The Queen's Colour

The Union Flag, in the centre of which is a foul anchor with the cypher of HM The Queen interlaced; above, St Edward's Crown surmounted by a scroll inscribed 'GIBRALTAR'; below, the globe surrounded by a laurel wreath, under which a scroll inscribed with the Corps motto 'PER MARE PER TERRAM'. The cords and tassels are of gold interwoven with silks of the Commando's colour which corresponds to the Unit lanyards worn by all ranks (see Appendix P).

The Regimental Colour

A blue flag with a small Union Flag in the canton nearest the pike head, and the cypher of HM The Queen surmounted by a St Edward's Crown in the other three corners; centre embellishments are similar to the Queen's Colour, except that the foul anchor is interlaced with the cypher of George IV and the Commando numeral appears below the motto. The cords and tassels are of gold interwoven with silks of the Commando's colour which corresponds to the Unit lanyards worn by all ranks (see Appendix P).

(See Illustrations Opposite)

The 40 Cdo Colours Party at the presentation of the unit's fourth Sword of Peace at Norton Manor on 1 April 2019.